Proving the Age of the Earth

By

Brian D. Shepherd, Master of Christian Education, B.S. Chemistry

TheShepherdFlock@verizon.net

ISBN: 978-0-9968079-6-8

All Scripture quotes are from the King James Bible.

The Old Paths Publications, Inc.
142 Gold Flume Way
Cleveland, GA 30528
Email: TOP@theoldpathspublications.com
Website: www.theoldpathspublications.com

DEDICATION

This book is dedicated to my Lord and Savior Jesus Christ.

Brian D. Shepherd

ACKNOWLEDGEMENTS

I am most grateful to my dear helpmeet, Phyllis, and to my two children, Adrian and Hannah for their patience, encouragement, and kindness toward me while I have studied, read, and written on these topics off and on over an eleven-year period. This project has often absorbed my attention beyond what most people would consider reasonable. Thank you for putting up with me.

Second, I am most thankful to Dr. James J.S. Johnson for his teaching, mentorship, friendship, kindness and humility as he shared with me many of the best resources for studying some of these topics as well as his extensive knowledge about the Bible.

I am likewise appreciative of all the other persons whose works I read, or personally interacted with at Institute for Creation Research including the scientists, Bible teachers, and my fellow students who were all instrumental in helping me and encouraging me along the way.

I also owe a big thank you to Dr. D. A. Waite for his helpful books and for his strong encouragement to get this work published.

Lastly, and truly most importantly, I am eternally grateful to my Lord and Savior Jesus Christ for allowing me the pleasure of getting to know His Word and His world a little better. I pray that I can serve well and represent Him as He would have me to do everywhere I go for the rest of my life.

PREFACE

Brian Shepherd has undertaken—and provided—a serious analysis of the age of the earth, carefully showing how to calculate (and how to not calculate) that timeframe. And, being no stranger to mathematics or Scripture, he has qualified his calculations with relevant tolerances (i.e., "plus or minus such-and-such years"), based upon the precisional information level of Scripture texts that provide chronology data. (Of course, knowing Brian's integrity and intelligence, I expected only the best.)

Yet this work begins with a larger frame-of-references than simple arithmetic applications. To rightly appreciate the analytical work that follows, the reader must appreciate the truth of John 12:43 (*"For they loved the praise of men more than the praise of God"*), namely, that too many people succumb to peer pressure as they seek the applause of humans, rather than seeking the approval of God. As the following pages demonstrate, the author is concerned with God's approval, as a scholarly workman reverently handling and rightly dividing the Word of truth (2nd Timothy 2:15), as he digests the chronology-relevant data of Holy Scripture. In doing this, he has qualified the rationale for his book's composition, including how he goes about refuting modern notions of a (supposedly) billions-of-years-old cosmos.

Because popular secular culture forcefully promotes an evolution-premised "old earth" cosmogony as an indispensable tenet of secular humanism, it is necessary to refute the assumptions on which this modern myth depends. Furthermore, many Christianity-professing churches have accepted the popular myth of evolution-based cosmogony, so evolutionary "ages" are also promoted via various forms of religious humanism, supplementing the misinformation promoted by secular humanism enthusiasts. Consequently, it is likewise needful to appreciate the many infallible proofs of Earth's relatively young age. The evolution-compromised/embracing religious humanism that inhabits many religious circles, and is even found in many "evangelical" Protestant circles, claims the Earth is billions of years old. Accordingly, this book provides critically important truth—supported by forensically relevant evidences—that can (and should) benefit the thinking of serious Christians, worldly Christians, and even non-Christians, if they have "eyes [willing] to see" the truth about just how old Earth really is. In order to help readers gain the value of this labor of learning, the author has included personal insights to contextualize and personalize the importance of this information.

The logic of this book's investigation of Earth's chronology (and its relevance to the larger picture, such as how the Holy Bible should be read and understood, and how the Lord Jesus Christ verified the Book of Genesis as true history, etc.), is carefully presented—the "why", as well as the perfectness of the Holy Bible (including its miraculous composition, including every "jot and tittle" of its original words as well as its providential preservation by God, so that the actual words of the Bible's original text have been protected and provided to us, etc.).

Because so many misunderstand the providential preservation of the Holy Bible's original text (in its original languages of Hebrew, Aramaic, and Greek), the author analyzes the common errors regarding Biblical text preservation (and transmission), including a ground-breaking analysis of the humanistic "scholar" villains who are largely to blame for our present quagmire of so-called "textual criticism"—which quagmire demonstrates the mess and confusion that results from ignoring Biblical (and forensic) standards for critiquing those who profess to be "Biblical scholars."

Having clarified the proper approach to recognizing, reading, and digesting Scripture's informative data regarding Earth's early history (starting from Creation Week, and continuing, detail by detail, into the New Testament chronology data), the author collates the Biblical data in order to clarify what the Scripture actually teaches about Earth's chronology (and thus, its age). The presentation is very methodical: from Adam to Abraham, from Abraham to the Exodus, from the Exodus to the destruction of Jerusalem, etc.—always analyzing what the Bible itself teaches about specific timeframes in Earth history.

The bottom line, mathematically speaking, is that Earth is between 6000 and 7000 years old, and much closer to 6000 than to 7000.

This ultimate chronology conclusion is then buttressed—after a brief review of some laws of logic (and attention to logical fallacies that sometimes distract from sound logical analysis)—with a sampling of corroborative evidences, including extra-biblical genealogical evidences, geophysical evidence (e.g., Earth's magnetic field), paleontological evidences (e.g., soft tissue in dinosaur bones), and historical/archeological evidences (e.g., ancient Chinese pictographs as forensic evidence of post-Flood memories of ancestrally transmitted pre-Flood history).

All the massive marshalling of evidence is funneled into a few salient conclusions, including recognition of how pervasively our secular culture "authorities" (and, sad to say, much of our religious culture "authorities") have lied to us about the age of the earth, as well as how accurately and precisely the Holy Bible has informed us regarding Earth's relatively young chronology.

Brian Shepherd has more than achieved his authorial purpose—to glorify God and to draw people to God and His truth. (And beyond that, the book's richly documented Appendix, exposing the villainous character of the so-called "critical text" promoted by counterfeiters Westcott, Hort, and their ilk, by itself, is worthy of publication!)

In Psalm 138:2, the LORD indicates that He magnifies His written Word even higher than His own holy name, so scholarship that caringly honors God's Word is to be highly valued. This book exhibits that worthy quality. So enjoy this gold-mine of research and analysis—you have a truth-treasure of pages waiting to engage your mind, and you will enjoy learning how *it's a young world, after all*!

James J. S. Johnson
Dallas, Texas (AD2016)

Endorsements for *Proving the Age of the Earth*

"Brian Shepherd has provided a serious yet very readable book of Earth's age, carefully showing how to calculate (and how not to calculate) that time frame. Because popular voices and crowd noises forcefully promote tales of evolutionary origins, this author soundly critiques humanistic "old earth" assumptions. He offers explanatory proofs of Earth's relatively young age (i.e., thousands of years old, not billions), to remove all justifications for accommodating evolutionary timescales. This book, containing Scripture, logic, and relevant scientific evidences, will clarify the thinking of serious Christians, worldly Christians, and even non-Christians, if they have "eyes [willing] to see" the truth about just how old Earth really is. **The Appendix alone, on the authenticity and preservation of our Bible's text, is worth the price of the book!**"

James J. S. Johnson, J.D., M.B.Th., Th.D., C.I.H.E.
Chief Academic Officer & Assoc. Professor of Apologetics
Institute for Creation Research
Dallas, TX

"Reading Brian Shepherd's *Proving The Age of The Earth* brings a clear understanding of the subject that is much needed today. Brian's passionate devotion to the King James Bible, combined with his scholarship and thorough documentation, has produced a book that is readable, true to Scripture and theologically sound."

D. L. Cooper, D.Min.
Pastor, Bible Baptist Church
Marietta, GA

(Please see the back cover of the book for other endorsements.)

ENDORSEMENTS OF PROVING THE AGE OF THE EARTH

TABLE OF CONTENTS

INTRODUCTION

According to a recent poll, most people trust television news more than they trust any other source.[1] Perhaps this is because people are bored[2] and have chosen not to read anything other than the lightest material (newspapers and magazines with lots of photos). People want to be entertained *even when it comes to the news.*[3] This is not the way it has always been in this country. An excellent illustration of the difference between people today and people who lived before the television era is a brief examination of how people were entertained 150 years ago. People did not live just for entertainment; they thrived on feeding their thinking processes. Neil Postman explained how this worked in his book, Amusing Ourselves to Death:

> "The first of the seven famous debates between Abraham Lincoln and Stephen A. Douglas took place on August 21, 1858, in Ottawa, Illinois. Their arrangement provided that Douglas would speak first, for one hour; Lincoln would take an hour and a half to reply; Douglas, a half hour to rebut Lincoln's reply. This debate was considerably shorter than those to which the two men were accustomed. In fact, they had tangled several times before, and all of their encounters had been much lengthier and more exhausting. For example, on October 16, 1854, in Peoria, Illinois, Douglas delivered a three-hour address to which Lincoln, by agreement, was to respond. When Lincoln's turn came, he reminded the audience that it was already 5 p.m., that he would probably require as much time as Douglas and that Douglas was still scheduled for a rebuttal. He proposed, therefore, that the audience go home, have dinner, and return refreshed for

> four more hours of talk. The audience amicably agreed, and matters proceeded as Lincoln outlined."[4]

A different sort of people existed then than exists today. Our present microwave society demands instant gratification, desires sound-bite-like answers to everything, and hardly knows anything about its own country, much less the Bible.

People Don't Read

Unfortunately, it is a bitter fact that most people don't read much. It was reported in 2003 that:

1. About 1/3 of high school graduates never read an entire book after graduating.
2. 42% of college graduates never read an entire book after graduating.
3. 70% of adults in the United States have not been in a bookstore in the last five years.
4. 80% of U.S. households did not buy or read a book in 2002.
5. Of those who read, only 43% read non-fiction.
6. Every single day, the average citizen of the United States spends four hours watching television, three hours listening to the radio and 14 minutes reading periodicals.[5]

These are startling statistics for a society that seems to think that it is the most intelligent, cutting-edge group of people who have ever lived on the face of the earth. And yet, we have an incredible amount of information available for people to read. It is estimated that there are approximately 130,000,000 different books in the world[6] and yet a successful non-fiction book only sells about 7,500 copies.[7]

The Reasons For This Work

With the above statistics in mind, I have attempted to write this work using extensive citations so that the reader can check up on me, but also to keep it simple, short, and to the point. Perhaps this is appropriate given what the Scripture says about sheep (to whom people are compared):

> *All we like sheep have gone astray; we have turned every one to his own way; and the Lord hath laid on him the iniquity of us all. Isaiah 53:6*

It has been said that sheep are dumb animals with herding instincts. In other words, they follow their fellow travelers blindly without thinking. If they have a shepherd to guide them, they tend to do much better, but it is quite easy for a wolf to catch one or more of them unless there is a shepherd to protect them. The point is not that we humans are as dumb as sheep, but that we are dumb like sheep in that we follow our own rules and the ways of our fellow humans so that we will be praised by our fellow man and fit in with the popular crowd. Is that the way we ought to be? Consider these passages from Scripture:

> *For they loved the praise of men more than the praise of God. John 12:43*

> *Suffer the little children to come unto me, and forbid them not: for of such is the kingdom of God. Mark 10:14*

God wants people to approach Him as little children or like sheep—putting their entire trust in Him rather than in man—seeking the praise of God and *not* of men.

It may sound like a bad idea to start out a literary work seeming to insult the reader by comparing him or her to a dumb sheep, but consider first that it is not me who says that, but it is the Bible that refers to people as like sheep. Second, this author is also dumb like a sheep by that same standard. Third, if you are reading this book, perhaps you are not as dumb like a sheep as some, because you might be beating the statistical data cited above (if you finish the book). Fourth, and last, perhaps we should all demonstrate some humility about how intelligent we really are.

With those thoughts in mind, I wrote this book as an attempt to reach people who have trusted in Christ as Savior, to build them up, and to edify those who do not know about these things in order to save them the time and trouble of reading all the books and papers that I have read on this topic. **Second**, I wrote this for believers who incorrectly think that the earth is billions of years old as a *beginning point* for their study on the issue. I have studied the topics covered in this work extensively over the last eleven years and I am convinced of what is herein, but the reader may need additional reference material and time to process the data to get to such a conviction. Realizing that, I pray that the Holy Spirit will open your heart and mind as you read through this short work, so that you will see the truth. Also, it is not my intent to hold myself out as an expert, but only as one who has studied a lot on this subject. As a sinful man, I acknowledge and expect that I may have some errors within this book. The more I study, the more I recognize how much I do not know. Nevertheless, perhaps some will find the information within this work to be edifying.

The **third** group to which this work is addressed is to that of the non-believer for whom the Holy Spirit would open his mind and heart. The Bible says that everyone knows the truth that God exists and that He created everything (Romans 1), but not everyone is willing to acknowledge it. For you, dear friend, I pray even more so, that you may know the peace, love and eternal life that my God has to offer. Before you begin to read, pray to God—even though you don't know Him yet, that He will allow you to see, because you are blind without knowing it until He removes those blinders.

Evolution?

As I stated earlier, this journey started in a serious way for me about eleven years ago, in 2005. However, I first became interested in the controversy between creation and evolution as a high school student in the mid-1970s when I was assigned a writing project for an English class which involved research and referencing, and I chose to research and write on whether evolution was true or not. I chose the subject because I knew it was somewhat controversial and because I wanted to gain a better understanding of what the argument was all about. Unfortunately, I didn't really learn much in my research, because my resources were limited to the family encyclopedia and to the local library (before the computer age), which didn't carry much, if any, useful evidentiary material supporting a young-earth or an old-earth. As a result, I ended up being somewhat confused about it all. My conclusion at the time was: Who knows whether evolution is true or not? I received an 'A' on my paper.

Then I entered a state university and registered for a biology class (my major was chemistry) in my freshman year. One day early in the semester, the biology professor stated very emphatically that if any student answered a specific question, on an upcoming exam, that the earth was thousands of years aged rather than billions of years old, a failing grade would be marked next to the student's name for the entire course. I remembered rolling my eyes and wondering how anyone could really know how old the earth is since no one was around at the earth's beginning who was alive at the time of my professor's remarks, and I also remembered that this same professor never defended his claim during the entire course.

Over the years, I engaged in many casual conversations with friends and acquaintances about evolution, the age of the earth, and the Genesis Flood. I heard people state various positions with great passion and/or conviction—generally supporting an earth that is billions of years old, a localized flood in the Mesopotamian area, and macroevolution. When I tried to engage in the conversations with queries about evidences, the answers were invariably the same. Examples included: "Well, everybody knows that is true!" or "It's the only thing that makes sense." Ironically, over the years, I have never met a single person who could really defend his or her belief, but since I didn't know what the answer was either, I was open to pretty much anything. In fact, for a number of years, I really didn't think it was very important to know the age of the earth and the universe.

But God kept putting people in my life who would make dogmatic statements about this topic and it started to annoy me that no one could provide evidence to support their claims. Oh sure, perhaps they read something in a newspaper or magazine, or saw something on television, but I thought surely people realize that television commentator's thoughts and writer's opinions are not conclusive proof. Then one day I prayed that God would show me the resources that would help me to see the proof one way or the other. It was a passive prayer. I really didn't expect an answer. In fact, as I was talking to God, I communicated to Him that since I really did not have time to research this topic, I would fully understand if God did not think it important for me to know.

Wouldn't you know it, within a very short period of time, I saw an ad in a magazine suggesting that if the reader would purchase three DVDs, then a book about 50 scientists who believed in the six-day creation would be tossed in for free. I only wanted the book, so I bought the DVDs just so I could get the book (this was back before Amazon, Books-a-Million, and other on-line bookstores made targeted purchases so easy, or at least before I knew about it). Ironically, it was one of the DVDs, which had nothing to do with the age of the earth that led me to one of the organizations that literally changed my life. The DVD was so good that I wondered about the company that produced it; I scrutinized the back cover and discovered *Answers in Genesis*.

Next, I looked up the non-profit *Answers in Genesis* on my computer and found that they had all kinds of resources about the age of the earth, the Genesis Flood and evolution. The following day, I called the company on the phone to ask if someone would recommend a video. The woman who answered the phone recommended too many options, so I asked her to narrow it down to one video. She put me on hold for a couple of minutes and then returned and recommended a video lecture by Ken Ham about WHY it is important to believe in the veracity of Genesis 1 to 11. That didn't really sound like what I wanted, but I bought it anyway, because I needed to get off the telephone and get back to work. The Lord knew exactly what I needed to hear and this video was it. Answering the 'why' question was a **major** issue for me. I needed to know why it was important to believe in an earth that is about 6,000 years old, why it is important to understand that the flood of Noah's day was global, and why evolution was not true before I invested my life into proving it to myself. In this Ken Ham succeeded.

In another example of God's prodding, I read 1 Peter 3:15 one day during my daily Bible reading:

> *"But sanctify the Lord God in your hearts: and be ready always to give an answer to every man that asketh you a reason of the hope that is in you with meekness and fear."*

For some reason (probably the Holy Spirit working on me), this verse managed to eat at my heart whenever I thought about the creation/evolution and age-of-the-earth controversy, and it drove me to action far beyond my intent. In the end, it changed my life, because the time I spent reading tens of thousands of pages, researching and studying over the next years was time that I thought I did not have to spare for such a seemingly "trivial" pursuit.

Next, I started reading books, watching video lectures, listening to audio lectures, reading information on websites and absorbing everything I could in my spare time. During this time, I discovered the *Institute for Creation Research* (ICR) (formerly in California, but now in Dallas, Texas). I started reading their articles on-line on a regular basis and then one day when I visited their website (2005), I saw that they were offering an on-line Master's degree in Science Education. I wondered if they would accept someone who had been away from school for 25 years, so I picked up the phone and called the referenced phone number. The dean answered the phone and offered to pray for my decision. No one had ever offered to do that before at any school that I had previously attended. As a result, I was motivated to apply to the school and was subsequently accepted. In 2010, the Science Education School closed after a court battle that ended with a biased ruling that was not based on the facts of the case.[8] I had completed between one-half and about two-thirds of the work required to obtain the Master's degree at that point. The next day after the announcement that the school had closed, I was invited to cross over and join ICR's School of Biblical Apologetics as a Master's student and to transfer some of my credits, which I did.

Later, I identified the *Creation Science Movement* (CSM) in Portsmouth, England and found more useful books and periodicals. The CSM is the oldest existing creation science organization on the planet and they operate in a country where only 2.5% of the population is evangelical.[9] They are truly one of the last groups standing firm to defend Scripture and true science in their country. This is the same country that was once the principle source of missionary work for the entire world. This is the direction in which the United States is headed unless a great revival occurs – one person at a time – throughout the land.

I pray and hope that God will use me as a center of influence in the second half of my life with regard to the creation/evolution controversy, the age of the earth, the global Noachic deluge, and with regard to the authority and truth of the Scriptures to reach people for the sake of the Kingdom of Christ. That is why I wrote this work.

Organization of the Book

This book is organized in a manner designed to cover key areas of importance, some of which may not seem particularly important to the reader until he/she has read the entire book. It is my hope that after finishing the book, the reader would understand why certain chapters needed to be included.

The first chapter's purpose is to explain why

the issue of the age of the earth is even worth thinking about. The second and third chapters lay down a foundation for explaining why the Bible should be trusted as the ultimate authority for calculating the age of the earth. The fourth and fifth chapter take a slight detour to build a very good, yet short, case for which English Bible should be trusted and which Greek, Hebrew, and Aramaic manuscripts can be trusted for source material behind the Bible in English. It also is meant to explain why other Bibles and manuscripts cannot be trusted for truth. This is important because much of the world is deceived about this particular issue. Finally, in the sixth chapter, the years are calculated using the Bible alone as a source. A range is given for the youngest to the oldest that the earth could possibly be. Next, the seventh chapter records a few pieces of genealogical evidence from outside the Bible, which generally support the Biblical record. The eighth chapter is a prelude chapter to the scientific evidences covered in the rest of the book. It is a light examination of how logic can and is often manipulated by modernists to achieve an end. It is a necessary chapter because many, many people fall for logical fallacies every day without realizing it (just by listening to the daily news on television). Chapters nine through thirteen are chapters that cover the various scientific evidences that support an earth, which is just a few thousand years old (not millions or billions). Even if a single piece of evidence were to be found incorrect, the reader would still need to refute every other piece of evidence in order to prove that the earth is as old as the modernists claim. I do not believe that is possible. The last chapter is a summation of thoughts. I have also included an appendix, which is a paper I presented at the annual Dean Burgon Society meeting in 2015.

I hope the reader will look up my references and check them. It is also sometimes a good idea to check the references given in the referenced books. In this way, the diligent reader will see that the claims made in this book are not made up, based on conjecture or bad logic, as some might suppose, but entirely on solid evidence, which conclusively points in to a single, unavoidable conclusion—that the earth is not as old as most museums, textbooks, and modern scholars claim.

Endnotes

1. Unruh, Bob; World Net Daily, "How Much Do You Really Trust the Big News Agencies?", http://www.wnd.com/index.php?fa=PAGE.view&pageId=339853 (accessed September 4, 2011).

2. *Cultural Marxism: The Corruption of America,* Matrixx Entertainment, Devon, Pennsylvania, 2010, DVD.

3. Postman, Neil; *Amusing Ourselves to Death* (London, England: Penguin Books, 1985), 113.

4. Ibid., 44.

5. Jackson, Robin; *Erma Bombeck Writer's Workshop, Some Startling Statistics,* 2003, http://www.humorwriters.org/startlingstats.html (accessed September 4, 2001).

6. Taycher, Leonid; Booksearch Blogspot, *Books in the World, Stand up and be Counted!,* 2010, http://booksearch.blogspot.com/2010/08/books-of-the-world-stand-up-and-be-counted.html (accessed September 4, 2011).

7. Jackson, Robin; *Erma Bombecks Writer's Workshop, Some Startling Statistics,* 2003, http://www.humorwriters.org/startlingstats.html

(accessed September 4, 2011).

8. *Institute for Creation Research Graduate School versus Texas Higher Education Coordinating Board,* Commissioner Raymund Paredes, Lyn Bracewell Phillips, Joe B. Hinton, Elaine Mendoza, Laurie Bricker, A.W. "Whit" Riter, III, Brenda Pejobich, and Robert Shepard, 2010, United States District Court for the Western District of Texas, http://www.scribd.com/doc/33449642/Judge-Sam-Sparks-Ruling-in-ICR-v-Texas-Higher-Ed-Coordinating-Board (accessed September 7, 2011).

9. Ham, Ken and Britt Beemer; *Already Gone* (Green Forest, AR: Master Books, 2009), 12.

CHAPTER 1

THE WHY

How in the world does one determine when something began and why does it matter? I know the day, month, and year that I was born. I even know the exact time that I was born. How can I know this? I know because I have a birth certificate that states as much. I also know because of the personal testimony of my parents, grandparents, extended family and some of their friends. Furthermore, no one has ever objected to the claimed date. I also have photographs of myself with date stamps on them, which were taken shortly after I was born, which clearly implies that the date is correct. Interestingly, I do not remember being born. In fact, I really do not remember anything about my earliest life. My earliest memory is perhaps from age three (and I am not quite sure about that age; I could have been four).

In the same manner, I am able to determine exact dates of birth for my parents, grandparents, and great-grandparents, based on their birth records, family Bible records, census records, and family testimonies to that effect. The fact of the matter is that my father has tracked our surname's genealogical history back to southern Virginia and northern North Carolina when my great, great, great grandfather, John Shepherd, was born (Virginia) and married my great, great, great grandmother, Temperance Epps, (North Carolina) in 1832. They joined Bethel Hill Baptist Church in North Carolina in 1834-35 (one of them in December and one in January). We do not have the dates that they actually repented in faith and trusted in Jesus Christ as Lord, nor do we have their dates of baptism, but we have good records on some things.

Why is this important to me? The answer is that it identifies who I am as a man. Not only does it trace my gene pool, but it also demonstrates my Christian heritage and probably why certain ways of thinking are the way they are in my family. Additionally, my family history bears witness to the fact that women bear children, seeded by men, who grow up to be men and women and repeat the process over and over again. It makes one wonder: if I was able to trace my roots back to the very first human parents, who were they and what were they like? Also, does it really matter?

There was a time when I thought it did not matter. This was something I alluded to in the introduction to this book. This may be true with regard to shorter-term family genealogies (a few hundred years), but there is a reason that it is very, very important if one considers it in the context of the bigger picture. The big picture is one which must be considered from the very beginning. If I tell you that, "In the beginning, I was born in Texas," you can immediately tell from the context that I am referring to the year of my birth and not some ancient time. You likely would also be able to logically conclude that because people do not live to be thousands or millions of years old, that I am referring to a time that must have been within the last century (or slightly over that if I happen to have lived that long). This is because everyone knows and observes that people do not live to be 250 years old or 2,500 years old in our day and time.

Likewise, "in the beginning" may refer to any number of situations. For example, in the beginning, this country's founding fathers unanimously agreed that the "militia," referred to in the second amendment to the U.S. Constitution, meant "all of the people capable of bearing arms"[1] and not just the standing army or national guard as some might try to lead one to believe today. The beginning in this case clearly refers to the period of time when our country was formed and specifically to when the Bill of Rights was being written or had been written.

Now consider that the Bible states in Genesis 1:1,

> *In the beginning God created the heaven and the earth.*

The first three words "*In the beginning...*" define something within a context. That something illustrates that before the beginning, time wasn't ticking. How can we know this? Simply because there cannot have been anything, except what God says there was (since he is the Owner/Creator and what He says is truth), before this beginning. Moreover, God has revealed that He has always existed and will always exist. In other words, He is not constrained by time. An entity cannot have *always* existed within time, because time is a limiting factor. That means the **only** purpose time can have is for man—God's creation. That starting place is the specified location that is known, where *the beginning* is defined as an absolute and certain point for the origin of time (as far as mankind is concerned).

To drive this point home, ask yourself, "For whom was the Bible written?" It certainly wasn't written for God's benefit. Nor was it written for his angels. The only context applicable is clearly that it was written for man's benefit. This defines the use of the term, "in the beginning," because it clearly means 'around the time God created everything—especially man.

Could "in the beginning" refer to something before God created the heaven and the earth? Of course not, because the written Word of God says the two are synonymous and God never lies (Titus 1:2, Hebrews 6:18). Once the foundations of the earth and heavens were laid and the beginning was defined, we then knew where time started.

If we further examine the definition of the word 'beginning' from thefreedictionary.com, we find:

1. The act or process of bringing or being brought into being; a start.

2. The time when something begins or is begun

3. The place where something begins or is begun

4. A source; an origin

Does it seem like I'm beating a dead horse? Perhaps, but this is very important. Why? Because some people think that, in the beginning, there was already something, and that time had been ticking away for millions or billions of years, or that it has been ticking away forever. According to some, in the beginning there was supposedly an infinitely small, compressed amount of mass, which exploded in a big bang. The problem with this, if it were true, is that we have to wonder where and how did the original compressed mass originate? Before getting trapped in the elaborate explanations for how the Big Bang theory might have/have not occurred, we must answer the basic origin of mass question. Mass is anything that takes up space, regardless of how infinitesimally small it might be. The origin of mass question is unanswerable by secular means except by pure speculation. Furthermore, the Apostle Paul makes it crystal clear to us that God is not the author of confusion by way of 1 Corinthians 14:33:

> *For God is not the author of confusion, but of peace, as in all churches of the saints.*

Therefore, we can know that He means the beginning was the beginning and not some analogical, dreamed-up story, supporting a humanistic purpose.

This might lead the reader to wonder why it is so important to understand all of this. Many, many people including theologians, pastors, professors, and leaders think this is a peripheral issue and has little to no importance. Is that true? Let's examine the big question that this book addresses: why is it even relevant to understand how old the earth really is? Believe it or not, the reasons are not all that complicated. We live in what is known as the postmodern age. Postmodernism has been defined as not believing in any absolute truths.[2] When people make up their own truths and live as if they themselves are gods (having the ability to define truth is an attribute of God[3]), they fail to be accountable to the one true God. By failing to be accountable to the Creator of the universe, many have deluded themselves into believing that scientists, academia and the media are more knowledgeable than anyone. Thus, they fall into line, like unknowing rats following the Pied Piper of Hamlin of literary fame, to their ultimate destruction.

The Bible states clearly in Proverbs 1:7:

> *The fear of the Lord is the beginning of knowledge: but fools despise wisdom and instruction.*[4]

Focusing once again on the word 'beginning' and understanding that the beginning precedes everything relevant to the topic of this book, it becomes clear that knowledge without the fear of God is either incomplete, invalid, or both. Additionally, it means that before there was (or is) a fear of God, foolishness prevailed (read the verse again to grasp this). Hence, postmodernism equals foolishness. Further, when one understands that the Bible holds truth as shared by God Himself, one must accept the entirety of it as truth, not just part of it. As a result, any passages contained within God's Word that allow men to calculate the age of the earth must likewise be truth. Any other assumption goes against God's own voice, for in 2 Timothy 3:16-17, the Scripture states:

> *All scripture is given by inspiration of God, and is profitable for doctrine, for reproof, for correction, for instruction in righteousness: That the man of God may be perfect, throughly furnished unto all good works.*

This passage warrants a close reading and not a casual look at the first few words. The very first word is 'all' which does not mean 'nearly all' or 'almost all' or 'some,' but every word contained within. **<u>All</u>** Scripture is given by inspiration of God or is God-breathed. Now that is something to think about. This means that modernists cannot, by definition, throw out inconvenient verses (proof texts) simply because they do not agree with them.

If this is true (and it is) then we must accept the Lord at His Word regarding every word and truth revealed within His Word. So, in this book, I will attempt to prove to the reader that God's Word is absolutely trustworthy, authoritative, inspired, inerrant, and sufficient for everything that we need as human beings. Then, from that God-breathed authority, we can derive some truths regarding the age of the earth. After that, I will present some evidential, empirical knowledge that fully supports our findings within the Word of God. After the reader considers the cumulative effect of the evidence, I believe he or she will agree with the conclusions presented herein.

Floyd Nolan Jones helps us to understand why this issue is so important:

> "...the contemporary view is that God has

> not protected the Scriptures, that they are not available in a pure form, and that this necessitates their recovery by reconstructing them from the Greek manuscripts which have survived to this day...Many Christians have been taken captive by the devil concerning the Bible manuscripts."[5]

The point is that if Christians do not believe in the fact that the entire Bible is trustworthy, then there is absolutely no basis for their faith in Christ's resurrection and for their own salvation. While believing in the absolute truth of the Bible is not a salvation issue in itself, understanding the Scripture's inerrancy and infallibility is critically important, because failure to understand God's truth as absolute truth will lead a believer astray and likely will cause him or her to have great difficulty with his or her spiritual maturation process and to enjoy the abundant life while alive. Regardless of how good the intentions are of those who fail to embrace the infallibility of the Bible, it does and will always open the door to further and greater departures from the faith.[6] I pray that the Holy Spirit may open the eyes of any readers who are blinded, so that they are able to read and understand this book. If that perchance includes you, dear reader, then pray for yourself—that God will grant you the ability to see His truth.

There are some who advocate that the sciences should trump the Bible. After all, should we not trust only what we observe with our senses in the present? Should we not approach an examination of ancient Biblical manuscripts the same way we do any ancient historical writing? At first glance, that may seem reasonable, but is it really? As Christians, we should acknowledge that we cannot know and understand everything. Thoughtfully regard this passage from Job 38:4:

> *Where wast thou when I laid the foundations of the earth? declare, if thou hast understanding.*

Furthermore, since neither Christians nor non-Christians were present at the very beginning, we must, therefore, make some human interpretations of the past. Secular scientists take great liberties with their interpretations, and when carefully evaluated it is quite easy to see that their end results are almost always a result of humanistic presuppositional thinking. With this type of thinking, the conclusion is based on the conclusion. In other words, their answers are based on circular reasoning. Young-earth creationists also hold to presuppositional thinking, but they are backed by the infallible Word of God. Secularists have absolutely nothing to fall back on except their own theories, which are based on assumptions of assumptions and so on (there is no end to it). Bible-believing Christians hold the Holy Spirit of God as their infallible guide to Scriptural understanding. Using a secular method to understand a spiritual book given by the inspiration of God simply does not work.

The correct view of Scripture is to understand that the book of Genesis is the foundation for the entirety of God's revealed Word to us humans; in particular, Genesis, Chapters One through Eleven, which explain the creation, the fall, the flood, and the division of the nations by language groups. If the creation (which includes all visible things) was not **very good** (by God's definition of very good (Gen. 1:31), which must be really, really good), then there could not have been a fall (when Adam and Eve disobeyed God and sin entered the world through man), because there would not have been anything from which to fall. Furthermore, if there had not been a fall, there would be no need for redemption through Christ Jesus. Evolutionist and non-believer Richard Bozarth explained it well in humanistic terms in American Atheist magazine,

> "Christianity has fought, still fights, and will fight science to the desperate end over evolution, because evolution destroys utterly and finally the very reason Jesus' early life was supposedly made necessary. Destroy Adam and Eve and the original sin, and in the rubble you will find the sorry remains of the son of god. Take away the meaning of this death. If Jesus was not the redeemer who died for our sins, and this is what evolution means, then Christianity is nothing."[7]

In this, Bozarth speaks the truth. He understands the reason we Christians must trust the Bible; a fact that many Christians do not understand. So, the point is this: if a person can believe that Jesus died and was resurrected from the dead, why would he or she have any problem whatsoever believing that God created the earth *very good*, that there was a subsequent fall due to man's sin, and that the reason we need Christ is to restore that separation of man from God, which occurred in the Garden of Eden (Genesis 3)?

Moreover, if the created world was very good in the beginning (and it was), then there **could not have been** any pain, suffering, disease or death prior to the fall of man. By anyone's definition (man or God), these things are not good. Consider that if there was death and suffering before Adam (and there was not), then millions of years of life and death could have occurred (evolution). This is why long agers cannot believe in the creation as described in the Bible without twisting its meaning or denying it outright. This is critical to understanding why the issue about the age of the earth is so important.

The principal issue here is about understanding the truth. Rob Bell, an 'emerging church' leader, wrote a book entitled *Love Wins*, which was published in 2011. Conservative critics claim that there are some heretical teachings within its pages, including the idea that everyone will eventually end up in heaven (hell or a lake of fire apparently do not exist according to Bell). I do agree with Bell that love wins, but an appropriate follow-up question to that title might be: exactly what does love win? Does it win lost souls to Christ? Perhaps, in some cases, it does, but only by the power of the Holy Spirit. Winning lost souls with false teaching is not winning them to true Christianity. A better book title might have been: *Truth Wins*, or perhaps: *Truth in Love Wins*. Of course, the material within the book would have had to be different as well.

David Kupelian, author of *The Marketing of Evil*, wrote:

> "...if you have a love of truth, you're never really satisfied with anything else. Counterfeit religious experiences and exciting escapes don't satisfy you. You're always hungry for real experiences, for a genuine relationship with God, for true repentance and change, even if you don't know how to get there. You want to know the truth about everything – especially about yourself. If you're wrong about something, you want to know it. If you've been living a lie, you're willing to see it – no matter what the cost."[8]

In a way, this sums up the objective of this work. I perceive myself as a seeker of truth. God has, in His grace, revealed certain things to me and I wish to share those learnings and convictions with other people in one brief book. Otherwise, I would be like a lamp that has been hidden in a closed closet for no one to see. What good is that? Now, it's time to examine how we can know that the Scripture is infallible and inerrant so that we may trust it for calculating the age of the earth.

Endnotes

1. Schultz, Daniel J.; The 'Lectric Law Library, http://www.lectlaw.com/files/gun01.htm (accessed September 17, 2016).

2. Gilley, Gary E.; *This Little Church Stayed Home* (Darlington, England, Evangelical Press, 2008), 24-25.

3. *Jesus saith unto him, I am the way, the truth, and the life: no man cometh unto the Father, but by me*. John 14:6

4. The Bible reiterates this point regarding wisdom in Psalm 111:10, Proverbs 2:5, 9:10, and 15:33, so clearly that it must be important since it is repeated so much.

5. Jones, Floyd Nolen; *Which Version is the Bible?* (Goodyear, AZ: KingsWord Press, 2006), 4.

6. Lindsell, Harold; *The Battle for the Bible* (Grand Rapids, MI: The Zondervan Corporation, 1976), 25.

7. Morris, Henry; *That Their Words May Be Used Against Them*, as quoted from the February 1978 issue of American Atheist magazine, (Green Forest, AR: Master Books, 2000), 375.

8. Kupelian, David; *The Marketing of Evil* (Los Angeles: WND Books, 2005), 239.

CHAPTER 2

THE INERRANCY OF SCRIPTURE

In an August 2011 *Newsmax* article, Jerry Newcombe quoted from a new book entitled, *Forged: Writing in the Name of God—Why the Bible's Authors Are Not Who We Think They Are* by Dr. Bart Erhman, professor of religion at the University of North Carolina, Chapel Hill, in which Erhman claimed:

> "...about 75 percent of the New Testament documents are forged."[1]

Newcombe went on to state that Erhman built his case on a foundation of Gnosticism, which traces its roots to the second through the fourth centuries. It should be noted that Erhman is also an agnostic.[2] Is there any way that the above quoted claim could be true? God forbid! Read on.

When addressing the issue of inerrancy with regard to the Bible, it is necessary to understand exactly which Bible is true. There are so many 'versions,' so-called translations, and paraphrases in the world today that it boggles the mind. It should be somewhat obvious to the reader that when God led men to write down His Word, the languages that were first used (Hebrew, Aramaic, and Greek) transferred God's meaning and intent perfectly. Some subsequent copies may have errors in them since they were copied by sinful, fallen men and yet we know that God's Word was inspired by Him, because 2 Timothy 3:16 testifies to that very fact. We also know from the Bible that God preserved His Word.

What might be less obvious is that God guided *believing* men to write His Word in their own words and did not inspire men to robotically transfer words from Himself. That means that God breathed His Word into existence through godly men – not perfect men – but men who believed in God's truth through His Word as absolutely inerrant and infallible.

And what of the errors in copies? How do we reconcile that with regard to God's promise to keep his Word pure in Psalm 12:6-7:

> *The words of the Lord are pure words: as silver tried in a furnace of earth, purified seven times.* ***Thou shalt keep them, O Lord, thou shalt preserve them from this generation for ever****.*

A little over a century ago, scholar John Burgon wrote that there are only four types of errors in Scripture copies: those of omission, trans-position, substitution, and addition.[3] Most of these errors are by their nature accidental. However, some are intentionally caused. Of the purposeful changes, there are those done in ignorance and those done with malicious intent. The errors that originated by malicious intent have led to a virtual potpourri of extant Bible translations, which are unfortunately recommended today by many godly leaders in ignorance. Let this be a warning to those who have hearing ears and seeing eyes. After all, Jeremiah 17:9 states:

> *The heart is deceitful above all things, and desperately wicked: who can know it?*

The wise should carefully study the history of the Bible and its translators, commentators, and copiers, and should not trust unregenerate men for the faithful transfer of God's Word through the centuries. We must look for the thread that connects men who are faithful to the Holy Spirit's direction in transferring His Word through the ages.

It all boils down to this: If the Bible is not trustworthy, then why should people become Christians and how can they be certain that they are saved from eternal damnation? Some scholars claim that we can cherry-pick what is true in the Bible and leave the 'questionable' material to the scientists and academics.[4] God forbid! On what basis could such a determination be made? Who is man to determine which parts of God's Word should be cast away?

One way that I have personally seen this manifested is by self-identified Christians who do not believe in Satan. In fact, it has been said that six out of ten citizens in the United States do not even believe in a literal Satan. Instead, they believe that the devil is a mere symbol of evil.[5] I once knew a senior pastor with a doctorate in divinity who personally told me that he did not believe that Satan was a real being. The reality is that it makes perfect sense to not believe that Satan is a real entity if one doesn't believe that the Bible is inerrant. What makes no sense is making a profession of faith to trust in Jesus Christ as Lord and Savior and then to reject His Word for humanistic reasons.

Some additional evidences of the Bible's authenticity include:[6]

1. Thousands of existing New Testament Greek manuscripts that were copied by hand over many years, which provides a broad base of support for the veracity and trustworthiness of Scripture.
2. Old papyrus documents from the second century, which are congruent with today's *Textus Receptus,* demonstrating accurate transmission of the text through the centuries.
3. The plenary text of the New Testament books was available to the believers who lived at the time of the Apostles and there is absolutely no record of

their being dissatisfied with it.

4. There are hundreds of quotations of the Scriptures on record by early church fathers, which is probably sufficient to re-create the entire New Testament if it were to be necessary.
5. The accuracy of almost all of the New Testament historical and geographical referenced material has been confirmed by scientific examination. Not a single error was found.
6. An incredible agreement exists between the various Spirit-led writers of the Bible down to the finest points, even though the books were written at different time periods and sometimes in different countries.
7. In the New Testament, there are at least 320 direct quotes from the Old Testament and many hundreds of allusions to Old Testament sayings. This attests to the authenticity of the Old Testament by the New Testament.

In the end, we Christians must believe the truth of the plenary Bible, including its history.

> "Failure here is always an indication of a departure from the true evangelical position."[7]

The Old Testament

How can we know that the Old Testament is inerrant? The answer is by the Word of our Lord Jesus Christ. Christ referred to the Old Testament on numerous occasions and stated in Matthew 5:18:

> *For verily I say unto you, Till heaven and earth pass, one jot or one tittle shall in no wise pass from the law, till all be fulfilled.*

And He spoke again in Luke 16:17 saying:

> *And it is easier for heaven and earth to pass, than one tittle of the law to fail.*

Jots and tittles are the smallest Hebrew markings common to that language. The text of the Old Testament was preserved through the ages by the Jewish priests and the scholars who studied the Scriptures.[8] In fact, the Apostle Paul acknowledged that it was the Jews' responsibility to preserve the Old Testament text in Romans 3:2:

> *...unto them were committed the oracles of God.*

The earliest scribes copied the Old Testament (after it was canonized - Genesis through Malachi) with incredible accuracy. As the families of scribes passed their copying work down from generation to generation over hundreds of years, the work eventually came to be done by the Masoretes (Traditionalists) around the sixth century A.D. The Masoretes were exceptionally careful in their copying work. They had very complicated rules for ensuring accuracy. For example, they would always count the number of letters in every scroll or book once they had finished copying it, and then determine the middle letter of the book. If the letter was not the correct letter, then the manuscript was destroyed. They did the same thing with all of the words in each book.[9] If the count was off by even one—on letters or words, then the book was destroyed.[10] The Masoretic text was what was printed after the printing press began to allow for rapid Bible reproduction and it is the best text that exists for the Old Testament which was written in the original languages (Hebrew and Aramaic).[11]

In 1856, a unique and godly man by the name of Robert Dick Wilson was born. As a young student, he decided to plan out his entire life and therefore determined to spend 15 years in the study of languages, 15 years more in the reading and study of the Old Testament manuscripts and related ancient documents with regard to those languages, and a final 15 years in publishing his findings.[12] Wilson eventually mastered 45 languages and dialects and read with ease from ancient manuscripts.[13] He compiled over 100,000 quotations from these various languages in order to illustrate and publish writings about the accuracy of the Old Testament.[14] He had this to say about the Old Testament,

> "...we have it with sufficient accuracy to be reliable as evidence on all great questions of doctrine, law, and history."[15]

And again quoting Wilson (as quoted by David Otis Fuller):

> "The results of those 30 years' study which I have given to the text has been this: I can affirm that there's not a page of the Old Testament in which we need have any doubt. We can be absolutely certain that substantially we have the text of the Old Testament that Christ and the Apostles had and which was in existence from the beginning."[16]

Much more has been written on the topic of the inerrancy of the Old Testament, but in the end, the conclusion regarding whether it is inerrant or not must revolve around whether Jesus Christ's own testimony was reliable since He appealed to Scripture so many times in His own teachings. Jesus Himself agreed with the idea that self-authentication is not normally sufficient in order to prove something:

> *"If I bear witness of Myself, My witness is not true. There is another who bears witness of Me, and I know that the witness which He witnesses of Me is true."* John 5:31-32

The reason Christ's testimony about Himself is

valid is because He was the only sinless man who has ever lived on the planet earth and since no one could prove Him to be guilty of sin, His Words could and can be trusted. Yet, He has two other witnesses Who can and do testify on His behalf Who have known Him since before the beginning—God the Father and God the Holy Spirit—the two other persons of the Holy Trinity. How can we know this? Because the Hebrew word אֱלֹהִים (Elohim) is the plural form of the word for God used in Genesis 1:1, *"In the beginning God* [Elohim] *created...,"* with a singular form of the verb "created." The only possible reason that a plural form of the word was used with a singular verb is to show that God, Jesus and the Holy Spirit were all present at the creation. Of course, there is a considerable amount of additional testimony that is supplied throughout Scripture, that the Godhead is in the form of three Holy Persons, but I'll presume that the reader already understands this as fact. There is also much other Biblical support that all three persons were present at the creation.

In addition to the affirmation by Jesus and the Apostles, the Old Testament prophets also testified over 2,000 times that the words which they wrote down were given to them directly from God.[17] So, if Jesus, His Apostles, and His Prophets knew that the Scripture was not inerrant and yet taught that it was, they would all be guilty of a horrible deception.[18] You cannot have it both ways. Either Jesus was telling the truth, or He was a lunatic or He is a liar.[19] In the end, the reader can be confident that he actually already knows the answer to this question. Paul makes this clear in Romans 1:18-20, 24:

> *For the wrath of God is revealed from heaven against all ungodliness and unrighteousness of men, who suppress the*

> *truth in unrighteousness, because what may be known of God is manifest in them,* ***for God has shown it to them****. For since the creation of the world His invisible attributes* ***are clearly seen****, being understood by the things that are made, even His eternal power and Godhead, so that* ***they are without excuse****...Therefore God also gave them up to uncleanness, in the lusts of their hearts, to dishonor their bodies among themselves, who exchanged the truth of God for the lie, and worshiped and served the creature rather than the Creator, who is blessed forever. [bold words are my emphasis]*

In other words, each person already knows and can see the truth of the Scripture unless he or she has already been blinded because of his or her refusal to acknowledge the truth.

The New Testament

The Old Testament text was written over a period of hundreds of years by many different writers, all moved by God. The New Testament was all written down over a 60 to 70-year-period by many different writers, all of whom were led by God. The entire Bible text was completed (both Old and New Testaments) by around 90 to 100 A.D. The dominant text that was used for the New Testament by the true church is essentially what is known today as the *Textus Receptus* (Received Text). Some of the churches that used the *Textus Receptus* (although it was not known by that name until the last few hundred years) included the following churches which existed in the first through the third centuries *Anno Domini*: all of the Apostolic churches, the churches in what is known as the Palestine area today, the Syrian church at Antioch, the churches of Scotland and Ireland, the Celtic church in Great Britain, the Gallic church of Southern France, the Italic church of Northern Italy, and the pre-Waldensian churches.[20] The *Textus Receptus* continued to be used by the great majority of churches during the fourth through the fifteen centuries. In fact, 99% of all extant New Testament manuscripts support the Received Text (about 5,210 of the 5,255 MSS available for inspection today).[21] When the great Reformation began, all of the churches that favored the reformation used the *Textus Receptus.*[22] Erasmus compiled the Received Text into a Greek text[23] side-by-side with a Latin translation. He chose from a plentiful selection of available manuscripts, which were available to him from all of the very best and oldest Greek manuscripts and a few Latin texts. He specifically rejected certain corrupt texts, which originated in Alexandria, Egypt,[24] which was a known center of Gnosticism, and he rejected the *Codex Vaticanus*, a popular manuscript that many scholars swear by today. The *Textus Receptus* was the base text that was used to translate from the Greek into the English King James Bible,[25] which is useful for all of the English-speaking peoples today. Almost all other modern English texts appear to have their roots traced to a line of corrupted texts through Origen and other Alexandrian sources (second and third century). These errant texts have transferred through the centuries by way of the Roman church (third century to present day), Westcott and Hort (19th century), and Nestle and Aland (20th century). Yet, these debased texts have been embraced by extant ecclesiastical leaders and have led to a virtual potpourri of modern Bible paraphrases (called translations or versions by most people).

Dr. D.A. Waite wrote:

> "Basically, I would like to say that the New Testament foundation or basis for our Greek New Testament which underlies our KING JAMES BIBLE was definitely authorized and

> accepted by the churches down through the centuries, attested by the evidence, and therefore absolutely worthy of being trusted and believed by us today or in any future age."[26]

William Ramsay, a Brit from the previous century with nine honorary doctorates and many other designations and titles, was considered one of the most important scholars of his day with regard to the New Testament. He set out to prove that Luke, the writer of the Gospel of Luke and the Acts of the Apostles, was in error regarding his geography and knowledge of the leaders in power at the time, and was in general careless with the facts in the Asia Minor district. Yet, in the end, Ramsay concluded:

> "I set out to look for truth on the borderland where Greece and Asia meet, and found it there (in Acts). You may press the words of Luke in a degree beyond any other historian's and they stand the keenest scrutiny and the hardest treatment..." [The Bearing of Recent Discovery, p. 89]."[27]

The most powerful testimony regarding preservation of Scripture comes from the Bible itself:

> *The grass withereth, the flower fadeth: but the word of our God shall stand for ever.* Isaiah 40:8

> *Heaven and earth shall pass away, but my words shall not pass away.* Matthew 24:35 [Jesus' own words]

> *...the scripture cannot be broken.* John 10:35b [Jesus' own words]

> *For ever, O Lord, thy word is settled in heaven.* Psalm 119:89

> *But the word of the Lord endureth for ever. And this is the word which by the gospel is*

preached unto you. 1 Peter 1:25

All scripture is given by inspiration of God... 2 Timothy 3:16-17a

One thing that I have noticed in all my reading on this topic is that most, if not all, critical text advocates have one thing in common, and that is, they fail to use the Bible itself to defend their wayward thinking. Yes, they do use the Bible to parse a verse and attempt to defend their interpretation of the Greek or Hebrew through their analytical criticism, but they never seem to invoke God's Word to vindicate their thinking; therefore, their assumptions must be flawed. With wrong foundational assumptions, it doesn't matter how fancy the footwork is to develop one's case—the conclusion may still be wrong. I've read thousands of pages on this subject from many different viewpoints, and I've never once found an explanation provided by these men about how they dovetail their conjectural thinking with the previous six verses (and others).

To conclude this chapter, let me reiterate that the Masoretic text (Hebrew and Aramaic) of the Old Testament and the *Textus Receptus* (Greek) of the New Testament do not have any meaningful errors, which means that God did in fact preserve His text as promised, and has kept it pure. As a result, it is completely trustworthy. The Bible is infallible, inerrant, authoritative, reliable, and sufficient for all our needs. We will consider more on these last three points in the next chapter. For those who claim that the *Textus Receptus* or the Masoretic text has an error or errors, I would ask, "Do you believe God's Word regarding His promise to preserve the exact Words within His Word or not" (see Matthew 24:35)? Whether you believe this or not, God's Word and Words MUST exist today just as it did when they were originally written. They must exist in Hebrew, Aramaic, and in Greek. If you disagree then you are either looking at the wrong manuscript or you are confused, because God cannot lie (Titus 1:2). With regard to the New Testament, I believe that the Beza 1589 edition of the Greek *Textus Receptus* is essentially God's original word, because I can't find any other source that proves true, and because I believe in the doctrine of preservation which is taught in God's preserved Word by way of the Scripture verses listed above and others.

Endnotes

1. Newcombe, Jerry; "The New Testament – Is It a Forgery?," *Newsmax*, August 2011, 48.

2. Noebel, David; "Letter from the Editor," *The Journal*, Summit Ministries, Manitou Springs, CO, May 2011, 2.

3. Burgon, John W.; *The Causes of Corruption of the New Testament Text* (LaFayette, IN: Sovereign Grace Publishers, 1998), 76.

4. Lindsell, Harold; *The Battle for the Bible* (Grand Rapids, MI: The Zondervan Corporation, 1976), 18-19.

5. Kroll, Woodrow; *Taking Back the Good Book* (Wheaton, IL: Crossway Books, 2007), 83.

6. Morris, Henry; *The New Defender's Study Bible* (Nashville, TN: World Publishing, Appendix 1, 2006), 2062.

7. Lloyd-Jones, D.M.; *What is an Evangelical?* (Edinburgh, England: The Banner of Truth Trust, 1992), 73.

8. Moorman, Jack; *Forever Settled* (Collingswood, NJ: The Dean Burgon Society Press, 1999), 7.

9. Ibid., 9.

10. Waite, D.A.; *Defending the King James Bible* (Collingswood, NJ: The Bible for Today Press, 2006), 26.

11. Ibid., 31-32.

12. Edwards, Brian; *Nothing But the Truth* (Faverdale North, Darlington, England, Evangelical Press, 2006), 358-360.

13. Waite, D.A.; *Defending the King James Bible* (Collingswood, NJ: The Bible for Today Press, 2006), page 35.

14. Edwards, Brian; *Nothing But the Truth* (Faverdale North, Darlington, England, Evangelical Press, 2006), 358-360.

15. Wilson, Robert Dick; *A Scientific Investigation of the Old Testament* (Birmingham, AL: Solid Ground Christian Books, 1959), 61.

16. Fuller, David Otis; *Which Bible?* (Grand Rapids, MI: Institute for Biblical Textual Studies, 1990), 44-45.

17. Lindsell, Harold; *The Battle for the Bible* (Grand Rapids, MI: The Zondervan Corporation, 1976), 35.

18. Ibid., 45.

19. Lewis, C.S.; *Mere Christianity* (Indianapolis, IN: Collier Publishing, 1960).

20. Waite, D.A.; *Defending the King James Bible* (Collingswood, NJ: The Bible for Today Press, 2006), 45.

21. Ibid., 46.

22. Ibid., 47.

23. Ibid., 47.

24. Moorman, Jack; *Forever Settled* (Collingswood, NJ: The Dean Burgon Society Press, 1999), 128.

25. Ibid., 175-178.

26. Waite, D.A.; *Defending the King James Bible* (Collingswood, NJ: The Bible for Today Press, 2006), 61.

27. Edwards, Brian; *Nothing But the Truth* (Faverdale North, Darlington, England, Evangelical Press, 2006), 367-369.

CHAPTER 3

THE AUTHORITY, VERACITY AND SUFFICIENCY OF SCRIPTURE

Pontius Pilate asked Jesus in John 18:38, "*What is truth?*" But Jesus had just answered that question in verse 37 by stating:

> *To this end was I born, and for this cause came I into the world, that I should bear witness unto the truth. Every one that is of the truth heareth my voice.*

Only the elect can hear His (the Truth's) voice. Those who turn their backs on Christ are blind to the truth as illustrated by Romans 1:24, "...*God also gave them up*..." All truth comes from God and He sent Jesus to share and clarify it for us.[1] For this reason, whatever God shares with the human race by way of His general revelation (nature), His special revelation (the Bible), His special theophanies (an appearance or divine communication by God to man), or by His prophets, must be true. This is because it is impossible for God to lie (Titus 1:2, Hebrews 6:18). Furthermore, what is true must be authoritative by definition, and the Bible is our only visible true authority today.[2]

Martin Luther illustrated the authority of Scripture in 1521 when he stood on trial under the threat of possible capital punishment for his views. He was asked to recant his writings and his thinking on a number of points regarding Scripture, but after sleeping on it, he stated (translation from German):

> "I am bound by the Scriptures and my conscience has been taken captive by the word of God, and I am neither able nor willing to recant, since it is neither safe nor right to act

> against conscience. God help me. Amen."[3]

Luther was not alone in making a stand for the Bible. Many evangelical Christians have made stands over the centuries, often paying the price for their commitment by death.[4]

Many prophets of God acknowledged the authority of God in their writings. In fact, almost 4,000 instances in the Old Testament refer to expressions such as, "The Lord spoke," "The Lord commanded"[5] or "Thus sayeth the Lord." In one example, King David, also a prophet, declared:

> *The Spirit of the LORD spake by me, and his word was in my tongue.* 2 Samuel 23:2

So, David made it clear that his own words came by the authority of God Himself.

In the New Testament, God the Father authenticated Jesus' authority in Luke 9:35:

> *And there came a voice out of the cloud, saying, This is my beloved Son: hear him.*

And, of course, as stated in the last chapter, but it bears repeating here:

> *For verily I say unto you, Till heaven and earth pass, one jot or one tittle shall in no wise pass from the law, till all be fulfilled.* Matthew 5:18

So, the Bible is absolutely true and authoritative. In fact, how in the world could Jesus' disciples have been expected to carry out the great commission of Matthew 28 (and by extension, how are we to do so?) unless the Scripture could be completely trusted and authoritative? The fact is that the Bible is trustworthy down to the minutest detail including the genealogies.[6] This is not to say that there have not been some copyist or printing press mistakes or some insignificant spelling errors that come up from time to time, but these errors ultimately have been corrected. Today we have an English translation, which was translated from the correct Greek, Hebrew and Aramaic texts—the authorized King James Bible. It is the best translation in English that has ever been made. Nearly every other English translation has a corrupt version of the Greek for the New Testament and a corrupt version of the Hebrew and Aramaic for the Old Testament as its source documents. The original autographs had no errors whatsoever and since God promised to preserve His text forever, we can bank our lives on the copies of the truest extant textual copies and on translations that are based on these true copies (since no original autographs exist as far as we know).

Many 'experts' today are trying to tell us that the Bible is not inerrant and that it takes human reason, popularly known as "reasoned eclecticism," in order to figure out what God's text really said.[7] Reasoned eclecticism is nothing more than religious humanism in disguise (and not a very good disguise). Would God hide His Word from His people and make it only available to those who are so-called experts? God forbid! God's Word says that He will preserve His Word forever; I cited several of the verses supporting that fact in the previous chapter. Here is one as a reminder:

> *For ever, O Lord, thy word is settled in heaven.* Psalm 119:89

The fact is that God has placed His Word at a higher level of importance than His own name and since God is truth (as previously explained), then the Word of God must be true as well and it should be revered. It also must have been preserved through the ages in order for His people to know His Word and He has said that He would do exactly that. How important is the name of God? Consider:

> Exodus 20:7: *"Thou shalt not take the name of the Lord thy God in vain; for the Lord will not hold him guiltless that taketh his name in vain."*

And what of God's Word?

> Psalm 138:2: *"I will worship toward thy holy temple, and praise thy name for thy lovingkindness and for thy truth: <u>for thou hast magnified thy word **above** all thy name</u>."*

God's name transliterated from Hebrew is Jehovah. Jehovah means "I am." "I am" is illustrative of the fact that God is, was, and will always be – He is eternal and transcends time. On the other hand, God's Word is also holy and is synonymous with God Himself which is proven by the fact of John 1:1, "*In the beginning was the Word, and the Word was with God, and the Word was God*." Later, in John 1:14, the apostle clarifies which part of the Trinity is represented by the Word—Jesus. This is a difficult concept to fully understand, so I accept it by faith that God, and Jesus [the Word] are one and the same (as well as the Holy Spirit—the third person of the Trinity). And yet, God says in His own Word (the Bible) that the Word (Jesus) is to be magnified above His own name. The Bible also speaks of Jesus being the Truth. So, the Truth and the Word are also the same (Jesus). Our Bible is the Word, not in the flesh, but in the sense that He reveals Himself to us through it and in the sense that Jesus is the only human who ever existed who epitomized absolute truth. A faulty Greek and Hebrew text or corrupt translation is not the true Word of God, but the true Word is that which was passed down from the original, which has been transferred over the ages through the Masoretic text and the *Textus Receptus*. Therefore, we should treat God's Word with the respect it deserves—perhaps not so much by being concerned about whether our Bible lays on the floor or not (Muslims require their followers to never allow their Koran to touch the floor)—but by reading it, understanding it and internalizing it.

Another question comes to mind: Is the Bible enough? In other words, is it sufficient to meet all of our needs? The question is not: Does the Bible answer every question? Consider the difference in these questions carefully. The Bible does not answer every question. For example, there are some things that belong to God alone,

> *The secret things belong unto the Lord our God: but those things which are revealed belong unto us and to our children for ever, that we may do all the words of this law.* Deuteronomy 29:29

But the fact of the matter is that the Bible does answer many questions and it probably addresses many more questions than most people realize. God did give us a mind to use and we are to use it to figure things out and to discern truth, but it must always be done through the filter of God's authoritative, inerrant Word lest we fall into apostasy.

> *For the time will come when they will not endure sound doctrine; but after their own lusts shall they heap to themselves teachers, having itching ears; And they shall turn away their ears from the truth, and shall be turned unto fables.* 2 Timothy 4:3-4

Remembering:

> *The heart is deceitful above all things, and desperately wicked: who can know it?* Jeremiah 17:9

> *The fear of the Lord is the beginning of*

> *wisdom: and the knowledge of the holy is understanding.* Proverbs 9:10

So, in summation, if the Word of the Lord is so important as to be placed by God Himself at a higher level of importance than Jehovah's Own name, and since God provided mankind with this same Word—His Scripture, then it *must* be sufficient for our needs because God is not capricious. He has a design for everything He does:

> *...being predestinated according to the purpose of him who worketh all things after the counsel of his own will.* Ephesians 1:11

The conflict between modern religious academics over the correct view of the Bible is principally one of authority. Is authority derived from a communal consensus (humanism) that arises from an evolving way of thinking or does it originate from God Himself? Many religious humanists believe:

> *"...the Bible must be interpreted by first understanding what its divinely inspired authors meant to communicate and the context in which they delivered the message."*[8]

The problem with this is that the original source of the Bible is God, so the correct interpretation must involve what God meant to communicate and not what His "divinely inspired authors" meant to communicate. The reader might think that this is splitting hairs, but in reality, modern liberalists are able to get away with their bad interpretations of Scripture and their affection for the diminished authority of Scripture by using this 'split hair' understanding. They also believe that they are smart enough to explain what God meant with regard to every passage in the Bible and as a result they often end up changing God's meaning because of their tunnel vision. In other words, instead of translating a manuscript, they often use what is known as 'dynamic equivalence,' which means they change the wording to tell you what they think something means. Real translating involves "carrying over" the words from the original language to the new language and framing the words as literally as possible as they were in the original language. Yes, words do need to be rearranged from language to language so that they make sense in the new language, but they should never be added to or subtracted from just because the translator thinks he knows best.

The 30-Day Month

Did you know that there was no October 5, 1582? Nor was there an October 6th that year. Why? This was because Pope Gregory XIII changed the calendar that year and implemented the leap year concept. The old calendar had drifted off by 10 whole days over the previous 1,600 years, so Pope Gregory announced that October 4, 1582, was to be followed by October 15th.[9] Why would the calendar need correction? Simply because a post-flood year is exactly 365 days, 5 hours, 48 minutes and 46 seconds long. Over time, the hours add up to a significant error. This means that you really aren't as old as you think you are, because every year when the anniversary of your birth arrives, the Earth is not in the same place as it was on the day/year you were born.

The fact that man has always been making fairly accurate calendars reflects his intelligence, which was given to him from the beginning by an all-intelligent Creator. However, our calendar today seems a bit inconvenient. Was it like this from the beginning? In a word—no. For proof, we turn to the book of Genesis and find that the precise days are noted for the flood of Noah's day:[10]

> *In the six hundredth year of Noah's life, in the second month, the seventeenth day of the month, the same day were all the fountains of the great deep broken up, and the windows of heaven were opened.* Genesis 7:11

Also:

> *And the waters returned from off the earth continually: and after the end of the hundred and fifty days the waters were abated. And the ark rested in the seventh month, on the seventeenth day of the month, upon the mountains of Ararat. Genesis* 8:3-4

Observe that the 150 days cited in Genesis 8:3 refer to five months, because the second month and the seventh month are specifically noted in the passage. We can count the days from the 17th day of the second month (Genesis 7:11) to the 17th day of the seventh month (Genesis 8:4) to get the 150 days.[11]

This one example of many elucidates the claim that Scripture is trustworthy as true, authoritative and sufficient. It verifies that the calendar before the flood was different than it is today and it confirms Genesis 1:14:

> *And God said, Let there be lights in the firmament of the heaven to divide the day from the night; and let them be for signs, and for seasons, and for days, and years.*

This passage states that days, seasons, and years are determinable from the heavenly bodies. In other words, our understanding of months (as an example) can be extrapolated by knowing how often the earth goes around the sun (which defines a year) and the fact that the earth turns on its axis (which determines a day). Adding the moon's phases to this understanding even further refines our understanding of months. Because the early chapters of Genesis explain such things, and because Jesus Himself authenticated Genesis as trustworthy, we too can trust it with great confidence for other calculations, such as determining the age of the earth.

Prophecy

One area that is specifically unique and has been substantially verified in the past regarding proof of the authority and veracity of the Bible is that of Biblical prophecy. Consider that a true prophet must always be correct in his predictions. He cannot make one single mistake. The prophets of Baal in the Old Testament were frequently wrong, which means they were not true prophets, but false prophets. However, even a false prophet can be correct on occasion, much as an analog clock must be correct at least twice per 24-hour period. Secondly, a true prophet must have gained his information from God Himself, because only God has the ability to predict the future—not one other person, angel, or demon has that ability.

There are more than 300 prophecies in the Old Testament that point to one single event—that of Christ's coming.[12] These prophecies describe in incredible detail the birth, life, death, and resurrection of Christ. No other person in all of history was able to match these predictions, and all of the predictions were made hundreds and, in some cases, thousands of years previous to their actual fulfillment.

One example of this is the prediction by Isaiah that Jesus would be born to a young virgin woman:

> *Therefore the Lord himself shall give you a sign; Behold, a virgin shall conceive, and bear a son, and shall call his name Immanuel.* Isaiah 7:14

This prediction alone is such an incredibly unique prophecy that it is incredulous that anyone could possibly think that it could represent anyone other than Christ Jesus. Yet, many textual critics refuse to believe that it is absolutely certain that He was born of a virgin. They like to suppose He was merely born of a young woman who was not necessarily a virgin.[13] What exactly is miraculous or prophetic about such a belief? Of course, absolutely nothing! So why would a prophet make a prediction that was to be a sign from God unless it was incredible—in a word—a miracle? The answer is that He would not announce an ordinary sign, because it would be totally meaningless. Sons are born every day to young women all over the world. A prophecy about a young unnamed woman having a son would be like saying "tomorrow is another day."

Some have alleged that Jesus merely orchestrated the events of His life around the prophecies He knew needed to be fulfilled, but how could an ordinary man decide the city of His birth or the details of His death? There was clearly a supernatural 'hand' involved in the writings of the prophecies of the Scriptures.

There are also a multitude of prophecies that have come true that are not specifically related to Jesus. One of my favorites occurred after the Babylonians visited King Hezekiah, who showed them all of his treasures. The prophet Isaiah then warned Hezekiah about the coming doom:

> *And Hezekiah hearkened unto them, and shewed them all the house of his precious things, the silver, and the gold, and the spices, and the precious ointment, and all the house of his armour, and all that was found in his treasures: there was nothing in his house, nor in all his dominion, that Hezekiah shewed them*

not. Then came Isaiah the prophet unto king Hezekiah, and said unto him, What said these men? and from whence came they unto thee? And Hezekiah said, They are come from a far country, even from Babylon. And he said, What have they seen in thine house? And Hezekiah answered, All the things that are in mine house have they seen: there is nothing among my treasures that I have not shewed them. And Isaiah said unto Hezekiah, Hear the word of the LORD. Behold, the days come, that all that is in thine house, and that which thy fathers have laid up in store unto this day, shall be carried into Babylon: nothing shall be left, saith the LORD. And of thy sons that shall issue from thee, which thou shalt beget, shall they take away; and they shall be eunuchs in the palace of the king of Babylon. 2 Kings 20:13-18

While this prophecy did not have to wait hundreds of years to be fulfilled, it did require waiting patiently for several years. However, Isaiah continued this prophecy in Isaiah 39:5-7, when he predicted that the Jews would return to their land after the exile period.

Fear not: for I am with thee: I will bring thy seed from the east, and gather thee from the west; I will say to the north, Give up; and to the south, Keep not back: bring my sons from far, and my daughters from the ends of the earth. Isaiah 39:5-7

After this, Isaiah made one of the most incredible prophecies aside from those related to Christ Himself. He named the future king who would allow the Jews to return to their promised land.

That saith of Cyrus, He is my shepherd, and shall perform all my pleasure: even saying to Jerusalem, Thou shalt be built; and to the

> *temple, Thy foundation shall be laid.* Isaiah 44:28
>
> *I have raised him up* [Cyrus] *in righteousness, and I will direct all his ways: he shall build my city, and he shall let go my captives, not for price nor reward, saith the LORD of hosts.* Isaiah 45:13

The record of this fulfillment is in 2 Chronicles 36 and Ezra 1. The incredible thing about this prophecy is that it was made 160 years prior to its fulfillment. How could Isaiah have possibly provided the name of a Persian king 160 years before this occurred? The Persians were not even a major power at that point in time. This prophecy would be similar to someone naming Barack Obama as President of the United States in the year 1848, when Zachary Taylor was President of the United States and Napoleon Bonaparte was elected the first President of the French second Republic. Yet, the Biblical prophecy came true, exactly as Isaiah said it would. Of course, the reason it did was because God gave him the information.

Fulfilled prophecies such as these help us to confirm the Bible's trustworthiness, sufficiency, authority, and truth. It validates the fact that the Bible is the Word of God and that you and I can literally bet our lives on what it says. As a matter of fact, you can bet your soul on it!

Endnotes

1. Kroll, Woodrow; *Taking Back the Good Book* (Wheaton, IL: Crossway Books, 2007), 102.

2. Lloyd-Jones, D.M.; *What is an Evangelical* (Edinburgh, England: The Banner of Truth Trust, 1992), 70.

3. Edwards, Brian; *Nothing But the Truth* (Faverdale North, Darlington, England, Evangelical Press, 2006), 97.

4. Fox, John; *Fox's Book of Martyrs* (Grand Rapids, MI: Zondervan, 1954).

5. Edwards, Brian; *Nothing But the Truth* (Faverdale North, Darlington, England, Evangelical Press, 2006), 98.

6. Ibid., 109.

7. Interview of Daniel B. Wallace on Textual Criticism, http://bible.org/article/interview-daniel-b-wallace-textual-criticism (accessed August 7, 2011).

8. Moore, Art; "Dumbing Down the Constitution: battles between 'living, breathing' and 'original intent' point to deeper divide," *Whistleblower magazine*, World Net Daily, September 2011) Grants Pass, Oregon, 38.

9. Finding Dulcinea staff (2011), http://www.findingdulcinea.com/news/on-this-day/September-October-08/On-this-Day--In-1582--Oct--5-Did-Not-Exist-.html (accessed September 17, 2016).

10. Cooper, Bill; "The Calendar and the Antiquity of Genesis," *Institute for Creation Research* (2009), http://www.icr.org/article/calendar-antiquity-genesis/ (accessed September 5, 2011).

11. Ibid.

12. Edwards, Brian; *Nothing But the Truth* (Faverdale North, Darlington, England, Evangelical Press, 2006), 76.

13. Wallace, Daniel B.; "Part IV: Why So Many Versions?" (2001), http://bible.org/seriespage/part-iv-wht-so-many-versions (accessed September 11, 2001).

CHAPTER 4

REFUTING THE DECEPTION, Part 1

It is now necessary to pause in order to build a streamlined case against what is popularly known as the Critical Text. The reason for spending valuable time and ink on this subject is that the majority of evangelical believers and nearly all of the cults, including the Jehovah's Witnesses, and the Roman Catholics use this Critical Text to "translate" their "bibles." Most people are simply unaware that there is more than one Greek text and more than one Hebrew text to choose from when it comes to translating the Bible. Not only that, but there are probably 50 different opinions regarding which view to take with regard to how to approach choosing the correct text. Of course, there can only be one correct view and that should be obvious to the reader if he/she has followed me up to this point. The view that filters everything through God's perfectly preserved, inerrant, and infallible text must be the correct view. This is because God does not make mistakes (including grammatical errors) and it is impossible for Him to lie (Hebrews 6:18).

The view that uses Biblical proof texts (the Word of God itself) as testimony supporting the correct text without twisting it to an unintended (away from God's intent) meaning will be the correct text. The view that honors God's Word and does not remove words from the text to make Jesus less divine and represents Him as having been fully man will be the correct text. The view that results in a Bible that does not add, subtract or change God's Word, and uses perfect Hebrew and Greek grammar is the view that leads us to God's true Scripture. While these two chapters are not meant to provide a thorough analysis of the issues, hopefully it will grant the reader a sufficient understanding of why it is so important to make sure he/she is using the correct Biblical text before proceeding with any conclusions about the age of the earth (or anything else). Let's look at the two principal evangelical views that are incorrect and examine why.

The King James Bible Idolized

While this view uses the correct Greek and Hebrew texts to get an excellent translation, the end result promotes the idea that God's Word was given by His inspiration in 1611 through the King James Authorized Bible. This is a twisted view of Scripture that buys into the idea that either someone believes in double inspiration (that the Greek, Hebrew, **and** English were given by the inspiration of God), or that God decided it was time to improve His Bible through Advanced Revelation.[1] This second idea is one advocated by some who do not believe that the Greek and Hebrew are even relevant anymore. These two ideas are spurious and are not supported by Scripture. Advocates of these positions tend to revere Peter Ruckman, Gail Riplinger, and other likeminded people. They put men's thinking above God and argue through a proof text such as Psalm 12:6, which states:

> *The words of the LORD are pure words: as silver tried in a* furnace of earth, purified seven times.

From this passage they twist Scripture to support their position by claiming that God meant for the King James Bible to supersede the Greek and Hebrew text because it has, supposedly, been revised seven times, or they may claim that the Greek and Hebrew texts simply are not particularly relevant anymore.

The problem is that nowhere in Scripture does it

say that a new language will be used to preserve God's Word. In fact, the word 'English' is not found in the Bible. The King James Bible is an excellent translation, but it is a **translation** of God's preserved Word, not the exact, real thing. Furthermore, if the King James Bible truly were advanced revelation, then how would you explain that God allowed His Word to become unpreserved in the Greek and Hebrew over the years from the first century to the 17th century? The fact is that He promised to preserve His Word, and that is not just the individual books of the Bible, but the very Words within each book.

> *Thou shalt keep them, O LORD, thou shalt preserve them from this generation for ever.* Psalm 12:7

> *Heaven and earth shall pass away, but* ***my words shall not pass away****.* Matthew 24:35

Another question one might ask is what Bible was the correct Bible the day before the King James Bible was released? I know the answers some of these advocates would give, and they do not work without some very fancy 'footwork' (Scripture twisting). Which Bible was the correct Bible in the year 1,000 A.D.? The answer is that God has always preserved His perfect text and it wasn't through the Roman Catholic Church as many evangelicals have been taught. The Roman Catholic Church traces its roots to the fourth or maybe the sixth century A.D. (not the first century) and it has done its very best, over the years, to burn every good text that existed. It wasn't until more recent history that they have changed their tack.

Now I am an advocate of the King James Bible. It is THE Bible I use in English and I believe that I can bank my life on it. I do not believe there are any theological or material doctrinal errors in the King James Bible. I believe that it is essentially the very

Word of God, but I don't believe that it is the God-breathed, given by inspiration text that God gifted to mankind. The King James Bible is an excellent translation. I believe it is the best translation for the English-speaking peoples, but a student of the Bible still needs to look up the Greek or Hebrew (and sometimes Aramaic) behind the English words in order to fully grasp what God is saying to us. For example, how could a reader know what the following verse (and many, many others) means without looking up the Hebrew behind the English?

> ***The LORD said unto my Lord**, Sit thou at my right hand, until I make thine enemies thy footstool. Psalm 110:1*

Only the Hebrew clarifies that the first "Lord" is 'Jehovah' and the second "Lord" is 'Adon(ai).' The meaning is that God the Father (the first person of the Trinity) is talking to God the Son (the second person of the Trinity).

The King James Authorized Bible is the Bible that was translated into English from the actual Word of God—what are known today as the *Textus Receptus* (Greek) and the Masoretic Text (Hebrew). Personally, I will not break fellowship with a brother who believes in double inspiration, unless he is militantly argumentative (and I have known a few who are), but I am inclined to break fellowship with those who buy into the advanced revelation concept, because they all seem to be militant.

The King James Bible was not available in the first century, the second century, and so on up to the 17th century. While some believe that it was, they do so by blind, and false faith. The Bible tells us to have faith that is supported by evidence.

> *Now faith is the substance of things hoped*

for, the evidence of things not seen. Hebrews 11:1

There is absolutely no evidence to support the spurious idea that the King James English Bible was available to believers in the 1st century.

So, in summation,

1. The King James Bible is not a preserved Bible from the first century.
2. There are no Biblical proof texts that support it as given by the inspiration of God.
3. The Greek, Hebrew, and Aramaic are necessary to clarify meaning in countless cases in Scripture.
4. The King James Bible is a translation.
5. The King James Bible was not available during the first 16 centuries.

The Critical Text

We will briefly examine four areas of concern here, because the Critical Text is the corrupt text that dominates the world today for use in Biblical translation and study. It has yielded a smorgasbord of paraphrases when translated into the English language (not to mention other languages) including the popular New International Version, the New American Standard Version, the English Standard Version, The Holman Christian Standard Version, the New World Translation, the New King James Version and so on. The Critical Greek and Hebrew texts are being used as the original documents for translating nearly every Bible in the English-speaking world (or have heavy influence in the notes) except the King James Authorized Bible and the updated, modernized 1599 Geneva Bible with John Calvin's notes (I won't get into the problem with that issue in this book).

The Critical Text is a very corrupt Greek and

Hebrew text that sources from unsaved men, fraudulent and corrupt manuscripts, bad theology, and humanistic methodology. Yet, this is what the majority of the world has been led to believe to be God's Word over the last century.

The four areas to be examined in this chapter and the next are:

1. The men behind the text
2. The method
3. The text itself
4. The theology

If the reader is unable to see the problem with the Critical Text after I address these four issues, I beg you to do some more reading on this important topic. Please see the appendix and the bibliography at the back of this book for some excellent source material that will explain this complex issue in more detail. Also, consider the possibility that you cannot see (understand) because you are not saved. The Bible says:

> *In whom the god of this world hath blinded the minds of them which believe not, lest the light of the glorious gospel of Christ, who is the image of God, should shine unto them.* 2 Corinthians 4:4

The "god of this world" is Satan, the master deceiver. Satan does not want you to understand all this. If you are unsaved, the only way to "see" is to change teams and get on God's side. If the reader is not saved from the lake of fire, then it would be best to pray right now to ask God to convict your soul so that you may see your sin and then repent in faith and trust in Jesus Christ as Savior. Once saved (or if you are already saved), then pray for the Holy Spirit to illuminate the truth about this important issue for you and it will be easy for you to understand (by faith [evidence of things not seen]).

The Men Behind the Text

The key men whom I have researched by reading their own words (including writings that are translations from Greek and Latin), are totally unregenerate (unsaved) men. I do not believe that God has left unregenerate men to care for His Word over the years. He has allowed sinful but saved men to participate in the preservation of His Words, but not men from Satan's team. God has even allowed some carnal Christians and misled Christians (about one thing or another) to be involved with protecting His perfect Word, but never unsaved people as far as I can tell.

There are five key men among many who have contributed significantly to the corruption of the Greek and Hebrew words of the Scripture. They are Origen Adamantius, Brooke Foss Westcott, Fenton John Anthony Hort, Eugene Nida, and Bruce Metzger. None of these men were saved (see the Appendix). I believe this is provable, but I do not intend to take up a whole lot of space in this book to prove it. I intend only to whet the reader's appetite to motivate him or her complete his or her own research if he or she is led to do so. Nevertheless, I have provided an appendix on this subject, which mainly addresses three of these men. Also, there are some Roman Catholic Jesuits who contributed significantly to the corrupt Critical Text. Roman Catholicism is a corrupt and perverted version of Christianity, based on works, so one might expect to find a perverted Biblical text in Greek and Hebrew, and that is exactly what we do find. One man, a Jesuit by the name of Cardinal Carlo Maria Martini, likely should be included in the list above (but I haven't researched his writings), served along with Bruce

Metzger on the modern Critical Text committee which brought us the corrupt Greek text that is used today to translate this text (called the "Bible") into the various languages. Other Jesuits who played a key role will be called out in the section (or in general) about the corrupt text itself. To get a very, very simple and quick grasp of why the Jesuits cannot be trusted, just do an internet search for "Jesuit + oath" and read the oath that they must swear by to become a Jesuit.

Origen

Origen lived in the second and third centuries A.D. He compiled a text known as the Hexapla. The Hexapla has six columns in it, of which the fifth is basically synonymous with the Greek Septuagint (a Greek paraphrase of the Hebrew Old Testament) and part of *Codex Sinaiticus* (an allegedly ancient manuscript containing some books from the Old Testament, New Testament, and the Apocrypha). This fifth column was purported to have been originally written before the time of Christ. Critics often claim that Christ and his disciples quoted from it exclusively. This is not true and has been masterfully debunked by Dr. Floyd Nolen Jones[2], Dr. H.D. Williams[3] and others. In fact, it appears that Origen created the fifth column of the Hexapla himself during the third century. In other words, he did not copy it from another source.

Origen was revered by Westcott, Hort, and Metzger, and is venerated as well by most (if not all) liberals, Roman Catholics, and modernists today. Origen was born in Alexandria, Egypt. It is historically documented that he castrated himself as a young man in the name of Matthew 5:29. Clearly, he was not a man guided by the Holy Spirit. He succeeded Clement as head of the Catechetical School of Alexandria, which was a hotbed of heresy. Origen was its third "president." Later, he spent time in Caesarea and then returned to Alexandria where he was subsequently excommunicated. He then moved back to Caesarea and founded his own school patterned after that of Alexandria. It is said that Origen wrote around 2,000 books. Some say perhaps up to 6,000. Today, only a hundredth part of his writings remain in existence and most of them are poorly preserved.

Origen was the first to teach that infant baptism applied to the forgiveness of sins. He was a Universalist. He allegorized Scripture *ad nauseam*. He was one of the first to teach purgatory. Jehovah's Witnesses and Roman Catholics alike cite him as a church father, but also many Protestants and even fundamentalists think Origen was a "good guy." His corrupt teachings and writings influenced a considerable number of persons then and now. Yet, it is believed that he was a major corrupter of Scripture in his day. He did this by adding, subtracting and changing Scripture—word-by-word and passage-by-passage.

Origen did not believe in hell. He wrote (all Origen quotes are translations from either Greek or Latin into English),

> "...let us now see what is the meaning of the threatening of eternal fire...every sinner kindles for himself the flame of his own fire."[4]

> "That the punishment, also, which is said to be applied by fire, is understood to be applied with the object of healing."[5]

Origen didn't believe that the Scriptures are literally true. He believed in the allegorical sense or spiritual sense, which is of Gnostic origin.

> "Many, not understanding the Scriptures in a spiritual sense, but incorrectly, have fallen into heresies."[6]

He didn't believe God created in six days or that God established Eden with a tree of knowledge of good and evil as stated by Scripture.

> "And who is found so ignorant as to suppose that God, as if He had been a husbandman, planted trees in paradise, in Eden, towards the east, and a tree of life in it, i.e. a visible and palpable tree of wood, so that anyone eating of it with bodily teeth should obtain life, and, eating again of another tree, should come to the knowledge of good and evil? No one, I think, can doubt that the statement that God walked in the afternoon in paradise, and that Adam lay hid under a tree, is related figuratively in Scripture, that some mystical meaning may be indicated by it."[7]

Origen stated that he believed that the critical link to understanding Scripture is through the educated.

> "...the 'key of knowledge' is necessary, which the Savior says is with 'the lawyers.'"[8]

Considering that Origen made it his life work to read, study, translate and write about Scripture, he could not have been saved based on his elementary, gnostic interpretation of Scripture. For if he had been saved and guided by the Holy Spirit, he would have easily understood these passages and many more that he failed to interpret correctly.

Furthermore, since Pope Benedict XVI endorsed Origen's works, that fact alone, makes him highly suspect as a reliable source for truth since Roman Catholicism is decidedly not true Christianity. Benedict *wrote:*

> "Origen of Alexandria truly was a figure crucial to the whole development of Christian thought."[9]

In the following quote, Origen is saying that he is of the opinion that Jesus was born before the creation of man and earthly things. In other words, He hasn't always been. But the Bible states:

> *"And now, O Father, glorify thou me with thine own self with the glory which I had with thee before the world was."* John 17:5

Origen also stated that he was not sure that Jesus was the Son of God. This reeks of a comment by a nonbeliever.

> "Jesus Christ Himself, who came, was born of the father before all creatures; and after He had ministered to the Father in the creation of all things...It is not clearly distinguished whether or not He was born, or even whether He is or is not to be regarded as a Son of God; for these are points of careful inquiry into sacred Scripture, and for prudent investigation."[10]

Origen claimed that there were seven ways to have one's sins forgiven. This is a bunch of baloney. Only God has the power and authority to forgive sins. There is simply no way to substantiate these claims from Scripture without twisting Scripture and Origen was very good at that.

> "...hear now how many are the kinds of forgiveness of sins in the Gospels. First, there is that by which we are baptized unto the forgiveness of sins. A second forgiveness is found in the suffering of martyrdom. A third is that which is given because of almsgiving...a fourth remission of sins, obtained by our also forgiving our brothers their sins...a fifth remission of sins, when someone converts a sinner...a sixth remission of sins, through abundance of charity...a seventh...through penance..."[11]

Origen said this regarding infant baptism:

> "The Church received from the Apostles the tradition of giving Baptism even to infants."[12]

Origen did not cite Scriptural support for his claim about infant baptism. He just made it up like he did many of his other doctrines. The Bible makes it clear that we may be saved only by believing faith and repentance. An infant simply isn't old enough to repent or believe. Baptism follows salvation. Enough said.

Brooke Foss Westcott

Brooke Foss Westcott was Professor of Divinity at Cambridge. He taught Fenton Hort (discussed next) and they became best friends (they were only 3 ½ years apart in age). He later became a bishop with the Church of England in 1890. Westcott and his sidekick, Hort, published a "made up" critical Greek text in 1881, using an 1800s version of copy and paste, from the most corrupt manuscripts including the *Codex Vaticanus* and *Codex Sinaiticus*. Many modern pastors and professors (even fundamentalist) defend Westcott and Hort as staunch evangelicals. Having read some of their works, I can state with great conviction that I heartily disagree. I do not think these men were saved. They denied the inspiration of the Bible. They denied the Bible's infallibility. They agreed with the false and unbiblical thinking of macroevolutionary theory. They worshipped Mary. They didn't believe that the creation account in Genesis 1-2 was true. They also did not believe in the preservation of Scripture. This despite Scripture's self-attesting to it by stating, *"Heaven and earth shall pass away, but my words shall not pass away"* (found in Matthew 24:35, Mark 13:31, and Luke 21:33).

Westcott stated outright that he believed Jesus Christ's life is what brought redemptive power to sinners.

> "...the parallel passage in the Epistle (1.c.) shews that the redemptive efficacy of Christ's work is to be found in his whole life (he was manifested) crowned by his death."[13]

This directly contradicts Scripture, which tells us that Jesus died and was resurrected for our sins. Westcott also revered Origen.

> "Never perhaps have two such men as Clement and Origen contributed in successive generations to build up a Christian Church in wisdom and humility."[14]

Fenton John Anthony Hort

Fenton John Anthony Hort was the more vocal and more openly worldly of the two (Westcott and Hort). Hort was professor of Divinity at Cambridge. However, they were mostly just two peas in a pod. They both wrote profusely and yet often wrote enigmatically (as many of these corrupt scholars do), yet there is much material in which we can find their lack of belief in the Bible and in the true Christ Jesus.

Hort and Westcott were involved in demonic activities WHILE THEY WERE WORKING ON THEIR OWN GREEK TEXT (but before the committee that published their Greek text in 1881 was convened).

> "...and I have started a society for the investigation of ghosts and all supernatural appearances and effects, being all disposed to believe that such things really exist...Wescott is drawing up a schedule of questions...our own temporary name is the "Ghostly Guild"... [Westcott] is preparing a companion volume for the epistles..." (Letter to Reverend John Ellerton, 1851)[15]

God specifically warned against playing around with the occult in several passages including:

> *"Regard not them that have familiar spirits, neither seek after wizards, to be defiled by them: I am the Lord your God."* Leviticus 19:31

Hort also wrote to his friend, Reverend Dr. Lightfoot in 1867, that,

> "...but you know I am a staunch sacerdotalist..."[16]

A sacerdotalist is one who believes that priests actually have special supernatural power and that they are the only ones who may commune with God. This is decidedly unscriptural (1 Peter 2, Hebrews 7, and others).

Hort didn't like evangelicals.

> "the positive doctrines even of the Evangelicals seem to me perverted rather than untrue. There are I fear, still more serious differences between us on the subject of authority, and especially the authority of the Bible."[17]

The fact is he hated evangelicals and he did not see the Bible as having authority over anything.

Lastly, Hort announced in this quote that he was not a saved man.

> "...the popular doctrine of substitution is an immoral and material counterfeit...Certainly nothing can be more unscriptural than the modern limiting of Christ's bearing our sins and sufferings to His death."[18]

Here it is laid out plain as day. Hort did not believe in substitutionary atonement. He was unregenerate. In fact, my studies of these men and many others who have been most heavily involved in the corrupt text over the past 2000 years, have proved to me that all of these men were almost certainly unsaved. Hort's "modern limiting" is not referring to limited atonement, which I don't subscribe to, but it refers to his belief in universalism—the idea that everyone will end up being saved.

Eugene Nida

Eugene Albert Nida was born in 1914 in Oklahoma. He majored in classical Greek at the University of California at Los Angeles (UCLA) and he learned how to translate by ideas rather than word for word. Later, he obtained a master's degree in patristics from the University of Southern California (USC). Patristics is the study of what are called the "early church fathers." However, these men (the early church fathers) were almost all the literary ancestors of what became the Roman Catholic Church. One of these "fathers" was Origen. Nida went on to get his doctorate in linguistics from the University of Michigan in 1943. It was during this time that Nida got involved with the Summer Institute of Linguistics and worked with Cam Townsend on the founding of Wycliffe Bible Translators. He also joined the American Bible Society to help them with translation problems. Nida's influence with these two groups as a man who became considered a world-class linguist, catalyzed the proliferation of corrupt translations into Spanish, English, and other languages during and after his lifetime. He also was personally involved with initiating a project to create a new Greek New Testament (really just a slight revision of Westcott and Hort's 1881 Committee's Greek text) after being influenced by the Roman Catholic Jesuits.[19]

This is where Nida did the most damage. It was his idea to translate from this new edition of the Greek

New Testament after it was completed, using a method that he coined, "dynamic equivalence." This meant that future translations were not really to be translations at all (translation means to "carry over" from one language to the other). Instead, translations were to be guided by ideas and concepts as interpreted by the supposedly all-wise translators. This ultimately led to the myriad of so-called translations that exist today in English. The truth is that they are not really translations, since they are not based on the truest Greek and Hebrew manuscripts, and because the translators didn't translate at all. Instead, they wrote out what they thought the corrupt Greek or Hebrew meant. This is humanism. The Holy Spirit was not present in the process. There is no possible way for mere men to consistently and correctly interpret a supernaturally originated (and preserved) document.

When Nida put together the team for the compilation of the new Greek New Testament, he insisted that a Roman Catholic be included with the group. This man, Carlo Maria Martini, was a Jesuit. He also had Bruce Metzger on the team whom we will discuss next.

David Daniels wrote this about Nida:

> "...after carefully researching this highly-respected man, I am afraid I'm forced by the evidence to view Eugene Nida as a Bible disbeliever. At every turn he has shown a lack of discernment, an uncaring attitude toward the holy scriptures and not a single sentence about offending a holy God. It seems the scripture is true regarding him, "there is no fear of God before his eyes" (Psalm 36:1)"[20]

Nida believed in evolution, he capitulated to the Jesuits, he fellowshipped very closely with the Roman Catholics, and he didn't believe that Scripture is inspired, authoritative, infallible, or authoritative. It is difficult to believe, considering the preponderance of evidence, that Nida was regenerate.

Bruce Metzger

Dr. Bruce M. Metzger was a textual critic, bible scholar, biblical translator, and New Testament professor at Princeton Theological Seminary. During a forty-six-year career at Princeton Theological Seminary (1938-1984), Metzger taught (influenced) more students than anyone else in the seminary's history, presented academic lectures at more than one hundred institutions on six continents, and delivered more than 2,500 sermons or studies in churches belonging to a wide variety of denominations. His book, *The Text of the New Testament* presented the essentials of what would later be termed "reasoned eclecticism," the dominant approach in the discipline today. Metzger had an influential role as a member of the editorial committee initially responsible for *The Greek New Testament* and later for the Nestle-Aland *Novum Testamentum Graece*. He also took a leadership role in the International Greek New Testament Project (1948-1984).

Metzger was well known for his involvement with the Revised Standard Version (RSV) and especially the new RSV translations. He was Chair of the Committee of Translators for the NRSV and was largely responsible for seeing it through the press. Metzger edited the condensed *Reader's Digest Bible* (1982). He took great satisfaction in the expansion of the NRSV to include all the texts viewed as canonical by Roman Catholic, Greek Orthodox, and Protestant Christians, and was pleased to present copies of it to Pope John Paul II.

Here is a quote out of one of Metzger's books.

Notice his double speak in the last line, but especially notice that he doubted that every miracle story in the Bible is true and hence he did not believe that the Bible was inerrant and preserved. Yet the Bible says, *"For ever, O LORD, thy word is settled in heaven"* Psalm 119:89.

> "There is also the possibility that occasionally early Christians transferred to Jesus whole stories of foreign origin. For example, the story of the demons going into a herd of pigs (Mark 5:1-17) is thought by some to be originally a non-Christian story that was appropriated by the early church and woven into an account of one of Jesus' exorcisms. It is obvious that doubt about any individual miracle story in the Gospels does not discredit all of them."[21]

This "story" about the herd of pigs was NOT just a story that was stolen by Jesus. It was an account attested to by Matthew, Luke, and Mark. This makes you wonder if Metzger had a problem with the miracles of the virgin birth, the death and resurrection of our Lord, etc... He certainly questioned the truthfulness of our Lord.

Here is another example of many in which Metzger makes it clear that he does not believe in that the Bible has been preserved to now, much less forever. This despite 1 Peter 1:25 which states, *"But the word of the Lord endureth forever."*

> "The Letter to the Ephesians presents a variety of problems concerning its authenticity..."[22]

Metzger didn't believe 2nd Peter belonged in the Bible. Yet, John 10:35 states that "...the Scripture cannot be broken."

> "Although the author of this letter [the second letter of Peter] calls himself "Simeon Peter, a servant and apostle of Jesus Christ" (1:1), and makes reference to his being present at the transfiguration of Jesus Christ (1:18), several features of its style and contents have led nearly all modern scholars to regard it as the work of an unknown author in the early part of the second century who wrote in Peter's name."[23]

Metzger made an appeal to the majority (above) when he said "nearly all" to defend his conclusion. This is a basic logical fallacy—to depend on majority opinion for determination of facts, which is a very common occurrence amongst textual critics.

Metzger proved that he was looking at the wrong Greek text (the Critical Text) with this statement,

> "Certain aspects of the literary style and content of the book of Revelation are noteworthy. The original Greek text is unique in the number of instances where the author has disregarded the accepted usage of good grammar and committed atrocious violations of the rules of Greek syntax."[24]

However, God doesn't make mistakes in His grammar and God is not the author of confusion (1 Corinthians 14:33).

Metzger was spiritually blind and clearly not a believer. He didn't even understand what Psalm 22 referred to (a Messianic Psalm).

> "...the meaning of the third line ['they have pierced my hands and my feet'] is obscure." (from the New Testament Oxford Annotated Bible by Metzger & May regarding a commentary on Psalm 22:12-13)[25]

The meaning is crystal clear to the believer. It is not obscure at all. It is a prophecy regarding Christ's crucifixion!

Metzger did not believe that the last 12 verses of Mark belong in the Bible (because they do not show up in the corrupt texts, *Codex Sinaiticus,* and *Codex Vaticanus*).

> "Whether Mark was interrupted while writing and subsequently prevented (perhaps by death) from finishing his literary work, or whether the last leaf of the original copy was accidentally lost before other copies had been made, we do not know."
>
> (Quoted from The Text of the New Testament: Its Transmission, Corruptions, and Restoration, page 228)[26]

We could go on and on, but I think it is quite clear Metzger was not saved. He was a humanist. Humanism is a denial of a higher power that is superior to that of humanity. It quenches the Holy Spirit to the role of an unimportant bystander.

Endnotes

1. Cloud, David; *The Mobile Phone and the Christian Home and Church* (Port Huron, MI: Way of Life Literature, Kindle edition, 2016), location 1742.

2. Jones, Floyd Nolen; *The Septuagint: A Critical Analysis* (The Woodlands, TX: KingsWord Press, 2000), 27-35.

3. Williams, H. D.; "The Character of God's Words is Not Found in the Septuagint" TOP Publications, http://theoldpathspublications.com/PDFs/Septuagint pdf, p. 21-26.

4. Origen, *The Writings of Origen: Ante-Nicene*

Christian Library, Translations of the Writings of the Fathers Down to AD 325, Vol. X, ed. Rev. Alexander Roberts and James Donaldson, trans. Rev. Frederick Crombie (Edinburgh, England: Kessinger Legacy Reprints, T&T Clark, 1869), 140.

5. Ibid., 143.

6. Ibid., 291.

7. Ibid., 315-316.

8. Origen, *On First Principles,* trans. G.W. Butterworth (Notre Dame, IN: Ava Maria Press, Inc., Christian Classics, 2013), 362.

9. Ibid., cover & flyleaf.

10. Jurgens, William A. trans.; *The Faith of the Early Fathers, Vol. I* (Collegeville, MN: The Liturgical Press, 1970), 191.

11. Ibid., 207.

12. Ibid., 209.

13. Waite, D.A.; *Heresies of Westcott and Hort (as seen in their own writings),* quoting from a commentary on the gospel of John regarding John 1:29 (Collingswood, NJ: The Bible for Today Press, 2004), 25.

14. David Cloud, *The Modern Version Hall of Shame,* (quoting from On the Canon of the New Testament by B.F. Westcott, p. 354) (Port Huron, MI: Way of Life Literature, 2009), 126.

15. Hort, Fenton John Anthony and Arthur Hort; *Life and Letters of Fenton John Anthony Hort, D.D., D.C.L. LL.D., Sometime Hulsean Professor and Lady Margaret's Reader in Divinity in the University of Cambridge, vol. I* (London, MacMillan and Co., 1896), 211.

16. Ibid., vol. 2, 86.

17. Ibid., vol. 1, 400.

18. Ibid., 430.

19. Daniels, David W.; *Why They Changed the Bible* (Ontario, CA: Chick Publications, 2016), 90-103.

20. Ibid., 206.

21. Metzger, Bruce; *The New Testament: It's Background, Growth, and Content*, 3rd ed. (Nashville, TN: Abingdon Press, 2003), page 159.

22. Ibid., 270.

23. Ibid., 294.

24. Ibid., 304.

25. Cloud, David; *The Modern Version Hall of Shame*, (Port Huron, MI: Way of Life Literature, 2009), 328.

26. Ibid., 326.

CHAPTER 5

REFUTING THE DECEPTION, Part 2

Next, we shall examine the method that was used to determine the Critical Text. Is it a methodology that is guided by the Holy Spirit or is it a method that is guided by speculation and humanistic thinking? The answer to that question should be quite obvious to the thoughtful reader as he or she looks at the following.

Over 200 years ago, a man by the name of Johann Jakob Griesbach (1745-1812) compiled a list of rules for determining which ancient manuscript reading was best or worst when comparing two like passages (a corrupt one and a true one) from ancient manuscripts containing Scripture. Some of his ideas were obtained from his teacher, Johann Salomo Semler (1725-1791), while other ideas were acquired from an essay (1734) by Johann Albrecht Bengel. Originally written in Latin, they are translated into good English here. These rules were first published in the Introduction to Griesbach's second edition of his Greek New Testament. My comments are inserted inside brackets and bolded. [Note: the misspelled words are from the original.]

The Method

> "1. The shorter reading, if not wholly lacking the support of old and weighty witnesses, is to be preferred over the more verbose. For scribes were much more prone to add than to omit **[how can he know this? There is no supporting evidence here nor has any ever been found to support this conclusion]**. They hardly ever leave out anything on purpose, but they added much. It is true indeed that some things fell out by accident; but likewise not a few things, allowed

in by the scribes through errors of the eye, ear, memory, imagination, and judgment, have been added to the text. The shorter reading, even if by the support of the witnesses it may be second best, is especially preferable - **[this is pure conjecture; it is not supported by any evidence whatsoever]** (a) if at the same time it is harder, more obscure, ambiguous, involves an ellipsis, reflects Hebrew idiom, or is ungrammatical; (b) if the same thing is read expressed with different phrases in different manuscripts; (c) if the order of words is inconsistent and unstable; (d) at the beginning of a section; (e) if the fuller reading gives the impression of incorporating a definition or interpretation, or verbally conforms to parallel passages, or seems to have come in from lectionaries.

But on the contrary we should set the fuller reading before the shorter **[for what reason?]** (unless the latter is seen in many notable witnesses) -- (a) if a "similarity of ending" might have provided an opportunity for an omission; (b) if that which was omitted could to the scribe have seemed obscure, harsh, superfluous, unusual, paradoxical, offensive to pious ears, erroneous, or opposed to parallel passages; (c) if that which is absent could be absent without harm to the sense or structure of the words, as for example prepositions which may be called incidental, especially brief ones, and so forth, the lack of which would not easily be noticed by a scribe in reading again what he had written; (d) if the shorter reading is by nature less characteristic of the style or outlook of the author; (e) if it wholly lacks sense; (f) if it is probable that it has crept in from parallel passages or from the lectionaries. **[this entire section is pure conjecture on the part of**

Greisbach]

2. The more difficult and more obscure reading is preferable to that in which everything is so plain and free of problems that every scribe is easily able to understand it **[God is not the author of confusion, and He meant for His Word to be read by the common people, so this spurious claim is outrageously wrong]**. Because of their obscurity and difficulty chiefly unlearned scribes were vexed by those readings-- (a) the sense of which cannot be easily perceived without a thorough acquaintance with Greek idiom, Hebraisms, history, archeology, and so forth; (b) in which the thought is obstructed by various kinds of difficulties entering in, e.g., by reason of the diction, or the connection of the dependent members of a discourse being loose, or the sinews of an argument, being far extended from the beginning to the conclusion of its thesis, seeming to be cut **[Greisbach is saying that only the educated have the authority and right to determine what is Scripture and what is not Scripture; he is absolutely wrong on this]**.

3. The harsher reading is preferable to that which instead flows pleasantly and smoothly in style **[this is an incredible statement by a man who didn't believe in the inerrancy of Scripture and who was not regenerate]**. A harsher reading is one that involves an ellipsis, reflects Hebrew idiom, is ungrammatical **[with this rule Greisbach tried to justify God Himself making grammatical errors, because he knew the Critical Text has many grammar errors]**, repugnant to customary Greek usage, or offensive to the ears.

4. The more unusual reading is preferable

to that which constitutes nothing unusual **[there is nothing in existence to support this silly claim with the possible exception of Greisbach and his teachers' wild imaginations].** Therefore rare words, or those at least in meaning, rare usages, phrases and verbal constuctions less in use than the trite ones, should be preferred over the more common. Surely **[notice this word of momentary partial honesty "surely," which gives the reader the clear indication that Griesbach was assuming his facts]** the scribes seized eagerly on the more customary instead of the more exquisite, and for the latter they were accustomed to substitute definitions and explanations (especially if such were already provided in the margin or in parallel passages).

5. Expressions less emphatic, unless the context and goal of the author demand emphasis, approach closer to the genuine text than discrepant readings in which there is, or appears to be, a greater vigor. For polished scribes, like commentators, love and seek out emphases **[pure conjecture]**.

6. The reading that, in comparison with others, produces a sense fitted to the support of piety (especially monastic) is suspect **[this is totally spurious]**.

7. Preferable to others is the reading for which the meaning is apparently quite false, but which in fact, after thorough examination, is discovered to be true **[it is difficult to believe that a reasonable person would actually list this as a rule, even being an unsaved pagan, but here it is]**.

8. Among many readings in one place, that reading is rightly considered suspect that

manifestly gives the dogmas of the orthodox better than the others. When even today many unreasonable books, I would not say all, are scratched out by monks and other men devoted to the Catholic party, it is not credible that any convenient readings of the manuscripts from which everyone copied would be neglected which seemed either to confirm splendidly some Catholic dogma or forcefully to destroy a heresy. For we know that nearly all readings, even those manifestly false, were defended on the condition that they were agreeable to the orthodox, and then from the beginning of the third century these were tenaciously protected and diligently propagated, while other readings in the same place, which gave no protection to ecclesiastical dogmas, were rashly attributed to treacherous heretics **[the truth of the matter is that the pre-beginnings of Roman Catholicism were planted in the third and fourth centuries A.D. and that is the time and place that many heresies originated]**.

9. With scribes there may be a tendency to repeat words and sentences in different places having identical terminations, either repeating what they had lately written or anticipating what was soon to be written, the eyes running ahead of the pen. Readings arising from such easily explained tricks of symmetry are of no value **[this may occasionally be true, but the rules that God-fearing scribes used included throwing away any parchment or papyrus that was found to have even a <u>single</u> error]**.

10. Others to be led into error by similar enticements are those scribes who, before they begin to write a sentence had already read the whole, or who while writing look with a flitting eye into the original set before them, and often

wrongly take a syllable or word from the preceding or following writing, thus producing new readings. If it happens that two neighbouring words begin with the same syllable or letter, an occurance by no means rare, then it may be that the first is simply ommitted or the second is accidentally passed over, of which the former is especially likely. One can scarcely avoid mental errors such as these, any little book of few words to be copied giving trouble, unless one applies the whole mind to the business; but few scribes seem to have done it. Readings therefore which have flowed from this source of errors, even though ancient and so afterwards spread among very many manuscripts, are rightly rejected, especially if manuscripts otherwise related are found to be pure of these contagious blemishes **[Greisbach assumed an awful lot of things; he claims to know the minds of the scribes from over a thousand years before he lived]**.

11. Among many in the same place, that reading is preferable which falls midway between the others, that is, the one which in a manner of speaking holds together the threads so that, if this one is admitted as the primitive one, it easily appears on what account, or rather, by what descent of errors, all the other readings have sprung forth from it **[more conjecture]**.

12. Readings may be rejected which appear to incorporate a definition or an interpretation, alterations of which kind the discriminating critical sense will detect with no trouble **[this is pure humanism]**.

13. Readings brought into the text from commentaries of the Fathers or ancient marginal annotations are to be rejected, when

> the great majority of critics explain them thus **[personal opinion a.k.a. humanism again]**.
>
> 14. We reject readings appearing first in lectionaries **[this is because they often witness against the Critical Text; Greisbach had no other reason to reject them]**, which were added most often to the beginning of the portions to be read in the church service, or sometimes at the end or even in the middle for the sake of contextual clarity, and which were to be added in a public reading of the series, [the portions of which were] so divided or transposed that, separated from that which preceeds or follows, there seemed hardly enough for them to be rightly understood.
>
> *15. Readings brought into the Greek manuscripts from the Latin versions are condemned* **[again, Greisbach did not like the Latin because nearly all ancient Latin manuscripts support the Textus Receptus and not his precious and false Critical Text]**."[1]

Later, in 1881, Brooke Foss Westcott, Fenton J. A. Hort, and their committee published a Greek New Testament using similar rules. Their rules have this in common—they are humanistic, reek of conjecture and have no valid historical reason for using them. Today, liberal (and many conservative) scholars continue to use these rules, although today they are pared back to nine rules.

Again, my comments are bolded and in brackets:

> "The following summary of principles is taken from the compilation in Epp and Fee, Studies in the Theory and Method of New Testament Textual Criticism (1993, pages 157-8). References in parentheses are to sections

of Hort's Introduction, from which the principles have been extracted.

1. Older readings, manuscripts, or groups are to be preferred **[conjectural reasoning, there is no support for adhering to this rule]**. ("The shorter the interval between the time of the autograph and the end of the period of transmission in question, the stronger the presumption that earlier date implies greater purity of text.") (2.59; cf. 2.5-6, 31)

2. Readings are approved or rejected by reason **[humanism]** of the quality, and not the number, of their supporting witnesses. ("No available presumptions whatever as to text can be obtained from number alone, that is, from number not as yet interpreted by descent.") (2.44)

3. A reading combining two simple, alternative readings is later than the two readings comprising the conflation, and manuscripts rarely or never supporting conflate reading are text antecedent to mixture and are of special value **[pure speculation that conflation ever occurred; the reality is that heretical manuscripts removed words and passages from Scripture]**. (2.49-50).

4. The reading is to be preferred that makes the best sense, that is, that best conforms to the grammar and is most congruous with the purport of the rest of the sentence and of the larger context **[if humanism is the determining factor, then it cannot be correct, Jeremiah 17:9]**. (2.20)

5. The reading is to be preferred that best conforms to the usual style of the author and to that author's material in other passages **[this involves** opinion, **which means it is**

humanistic]. (2.20)

6. The reading is to be preferred that most fitly explains the existence of the others **[this rule makes sense on the surface, but if God said it and it does not make sense to the reader then either the reader is unsaved or not ready to understand]**. *(2.22-23)*

7. The reading is less likely to be original that combines the appearance of an improvement in the sense with the absence of its reality **[again this is not something for the scholar to determine; only God determines true Scripture. If it does not make sense then perhaps the reader needs to pray for wisdom (James 1:5) or grow spiritually]**; the scribal alteration will have an apparent excellence, while the original will have the highest real excellence **[humanism]**. (2.27, 29)

8. The reading is less likely to be original that shows a disposition to smooth away difficulties (another way of stating that the harder reading is preferable). (2.28) **[this is simply a ridiculous speculation]**

9. Readings are to be preferred that are found in a manuscript that habitually contains superior readings as determined by intrinsic and transcriptional probability **[note the word 'probability' here; this is an unwitting confession by the textual critics that their entire system is corrupt and based entirely on their own conjecture and humanistic thinking]**. Certainty is increased if such a better manuscript is found also to be an older manuscript **[older is not always an indication of quality]** (2.32-33) and if such a manuscript habitually contains reading that prove themselves antecedent to mixture and

> independent of external contamination by other, inferior texts (2.150-51). The same principles apply to groups of manuscripts (2.260-61)."[2]

As the reader can see, the rules that Greisbach and Westcott and Hort used long ago are very, very similar to what are used by modern textual critics today to "determine" which ancient manuscripts are true Scripture readings. Their humanistic means of interpretation is defended by their assuming that God-given inspired Scripture may be justifiably evaluated just like any other ancient secular book. Humanism is a way of thinking that takes the Holy Spirit of God completely and totally out of the equation. According to their way of thinking, all decisions regarding which texts are correct are to be made by educated men and women, who supposedly know best. In this way, they determine for the rest of the world what they think Scripture says. This is clearly a deeply flawed methodology.

The Text

The next area of interest is an examination of the text itself. The textual critics claim their best source manuscripts for the Scriptures are *Codex Vaticanus and Codex Sinaiticus*. Their "battle cry" is that these documents are the "oldest and best" manuscripts. I cannot tell you how many times I have heard or read that phrase from those who have drunk the critics Kool-Aid. The liberal critics claim that the two codices mentioned above are dated to the fourth century Anno Domini (A.D.), which would make them very old if it were true. They also claim as fact that the older a manuscript is, the more trustworthy it is to the scholar.

The problem is that these codices and some others that support the critical text are almost certainly not as old as they claim and they are not trustworthy at all. The fact of the matter is that there is very good evidence that both of their "precious" supporting manuscripts date to the 15th and 19th centuries and are poor forgeries. This fact is well established and argued in a video by Adullam Films (Bridge to Babylon)[3] and in a wonderful and highly recommended scholarly book by William Cooper entitled, The Forging of Codex Sinaiticus.

The source for *Codex Sinaiticus* traces to the 1830s, when a young Greek paleographer by the name of Constantine Simonides was hired to copy various manuscripts onto an existing, nearly blank, stock book of parchment, which had been sitting around for a number of years (perhaps decades, but not centuries). He was told that his copy was to be gifted to the Czar of Russia. Simonides had no real knowledge of Scripture (which explains why he did not notice some important differences in the Greek text he copied), but he was an excellent copyist, so he took a great deal of time to copy Greek letter after Greek letter onto hundreds of parchment pages for what he thought was to be a gift to the Czar. Later, he learned that the book had never been given to the Czar, but that it had been inserted into the library at Mount Sinai.[4] In fact, it appears that the Jesuits, who apparently controlled the project, never intended for the book to go to the Czar in the first place.

After he found out that it had not yet been sent to the Czar, Simonides visited the library at Mt. Sinai and asked to examine the Codex. The librarian shared it with him and he discovered that it had the appearance of having been artificially aged and that the dedication to the Czar had been removed. Then in 1844, Constantin Tischendorf showed up at the library and later claimed that he had found some of the sheets from the Codex in question in a wastebasket waiting to be burned. This was after the 'hook' had been set by the Roman Catholic Jesuits by allowing him to view *Codex Vaticanus* in Rome. This Codex was also almost certainly a forgery in the sense that it was grossly misdated to the 4th century A.D., when in truth it is very likely a 15th century creation. For Roman Catholics to allow a Protestant onto their turf to view these two allegedly ancient texts is beyond the pale in ridiculousness. The Pope at that time, Gregory XVI, was extremely anti-true-Christian and very hands-on with regard to having certain persons eliminated who did not agree with his thinking (he lacked certain character traits that one would expect from a man who had trusted in Christ as his Savior). In fact, he personally issued 110 death sentences for those who disagreed with him. He even had a man beheaded during the very year that Tischendorf visited him. Imagine that. The young, not-at-all-famous-at-the-time, unimportant, non-Catholic (Lutheran), Constantin Tischendorf, managed to gain a personal audience with the Pope himself in 1843.[5]

Pope Gregory XVI hated non-Catholics with great earnestness. He had people who disagreed with his policies bound up and inserted into openings in large stone walls while they were alive. These non-conformists were closed into the wall with stone and mortar and then left to die inside the walls, only to be found a few years later (1849) by Garibaldi, who overthrew Rome. He then opened the dungeons and tore down the walls for all the world to see. It was also discovered that the Pope, during his term in office, had certain enemies inserted alive into ovens to be burned, among other atrocities.[6]

The Jesuits, it seems, had befriended Constantin Tischendorf, funded his expedition, facilitated his meeting with the Pope, and guided him to the supposedly ancient manuscripts that they wanted him to see and/or discover for himself. No Lutheran, Protestant, or Christian of any variety had ever been allowed near the Vatican Library or the Library at Sinai before this time as far as is known. Yet, Cardinal Mai, a Jesuit, arranged for Tischendorf to see *Codex Vaticanus* in Rome and to 'find' *Codex Sinaiticus* at a monastery. The likely reason that the Jesuits arranged for the discovery of a second manuscript was to authenticate it as a witness to the dubious *Codex Vaticanus.*[7] The problem with that is that both documents are so corrupt they disagree between themselves in over 3,000 places in the gospels alone.

Furthermore, both codices use classical Greek in some places and Koine Greek in other places (used in two distinctly different periods of time). This inconsistency alone gives supporters of the Critical Text a major headache because they cannot justify why this could have occurred, and they mostly do not try. They simply ignore the problem.

Vaticanus leaves out 1,491 words or phrases in the gospels alone. Both documents use parts of the spurious Septuagint, a Greek translation of the Hebrew Old Testament.[8] Some parts are copied from 19th century Latin that has been translated to Greek. This is clear because of the words and phrases used, which were not in use in the 4th century. Dr. Bill Cooper explains with regard to *Sinaiticus*:

> If ever evidence were needed for the 19th-century composition of Codex Sinaiticus, it is surely this, that the Greek of the apocryphal Shepherd of Hermas that is bound in with the Codex - and is the same age and provenance as the Codex - and is even written on the same vellum and in the same ink as the rest of the

> Codex - is written in what is essentially modern (i.e. medieval to 19th-century) Greek.[9]

Cooper goes on:

> ...its grammar, syntax and vocabulary together shouted out the fact that it was written in modern and not in ancient Greek. It was one of the most audacious acts of dishonesty and sleight of hand ever perpetrated on the academic world, and the real wonder is that he [Tischendorf] was allowed to get away with it. But instead of condemning his dishonesty, almost the entire academic world closed its ranks about him and agreed with him. There was too much at stake for it to do otherwise.[10]

We can also know with reasonable certainty that *Codex Vaticanus* was written out in Rome (or under the control of the Vatican) before its "discovery," because the personal names that are spelled out in *Vaticanus* are spelled as they appear in the Romish Latin Vulgate and not like any Greek language manuscript would spell them. Also, the chapter divisions are done just like the Vulgate, not like any true Greek manuscript. Even Westcott and Hort conceded that the *Vaticanus* and *Sinaiticus* codices were almost certainly written in Rome and not in Alexandria, Egypt.[11]

Codex Vaticanus was "discovered" in 1475. Desiderius Erasmus of Rotterdam looked at it in the early 1500s and found it lacking in integrity. The Vatican needed another witness to make the codex legitimate because Erasmus' rejection was sort of a 'kiss of death,' since he was considered one of the most intelligent men in Europe in the 1500s. It appears that Jesuits conceived a plan to authenticate *Codex Vaticanus* as genuine in the 1800s by bringing *Codex Sinaiticus* into existence. All they needed was to get a non-Catholic to buy into the fraud. They found a willing enabler in the young, fame-seeking Constantin Tischendorf, and the rest is history.[12]

There are a considerable number of reasons that we can know with near certainty that *Codex Sinaiticus* is a fraud. I'll name just a few here. First, we have the testimony of Constantine Simonides that he was hired in the 1800s to copy out the codex. Second, artificial aging of parchment to the degree of 15 centuries is simply not possible and it is quite clear by examining the condition of the pages today that it is not that old. Microscopic studies of the parchment indicate that the parchment has the consistency both of calf skin and sheep skin within the various pages. Today, the pages do not have the major discoloring that always occurs on calf skin and/or sheep skin that is that old. The pages are not cracked and brittle as an ancient skin would be expected to be—they are quite supple and they show little sign of oxidation. Parchment, or animal skin, has the protein collagen in it. As it deteriorates, the parchment would have lost its suppleness.[13] This is simply not the case with *Codex Sinaiticus* or *Codex Vaticanus*. These two things by themselves should be enough to convince any reasonable person of the fraud involved, but there is much, much more evidence clearly pointing out the deceit that the Jesuits apparently gifted to the world through these two codices.

Additionally, there are the square worm holes. There are the cut outs, and the obvious symmetrical tears to remove Simonides' personal codes which authenticated his authorship. There is the modern Greek (not Greek from the first century). There is the Latinized Greek, which is not Greek at all. There is purposeful smearing and staining on page after page, that does not match up with other pages, clearing indicating there was a malicious intent to artificially age the manuscript page by page. There are the multiple round, worm holes that only go through one page and never through two together. Lastly, there is the Vatican's own record and admission of forging documents through the ages.[14] Other examples include:

> All these facts about the spurious nature of the Donation [of Constantine] are readily admitted to by the Vatican. There'd be little point in denying them. Yet the Donation is not the only notorious forgery that the Vatican has committed, and to which it cheerfully admits. Just some of the others, all of them political claims of sovereignty, include: The Apostolic Constitutions; The Apostolic Canons; The Liber Pontificalis; The Letter of St Peter; The Vita Beati Sylvestri; The Gesta Sylvestri; The Constitutum Sylvestri; The Symmachian Forgeries; The Decretals of Isidore; The Decretum of Gratian, and so on. There are many, many others. Then there are innumerable saints' lives and relics, all of them forged, by which they have deceived the whole world. And it hasn't stopped even today.[15]

All this and more is explained in wonderful detail in Bill Cooper's fine work, *The Forging of Codex Sinaiticus*. Anyone who ignores the evidence does so at his own peril. When choosing a Greek and Hebrew text for a foundational document to translate from into the various languages, the modern United Bible Societies Greek text is clearly based on fraudulent manuscripts.

The Theology

The last thing to examine is the theology of the textual critics. I've stated previously that textual critics never (as far as I anything I have ever read) use Bible content to back up their arguments. This is because they do not agree with 2 Timothy 3:16 which states,

> *All scripture is given by inspiration of God,*

and is profitable for doctrine, for reproof, for correction, for instruction in righteousness:

'All Scripture' is an incredibly high standard. It means every single Word is given by the inspiration of God. Second, textual critics, in general, do not agree that Scripture's very Words have always been and will always be preserved by God Himself. Critics will make arguments that they do agree with these two points, but then they'll turn around and contradict themselves. Many will agree that Scripture was given by the inspiration of God back when it was first written down, but that it was not preserved through the ages. They argue that anyone who stands against them must produce the preserved text.

Personally, I believe that the preserved Hebrew text is the Masoretic text, Daniel Bomberg edition, edited by Ben Chayyim (1524-25 A.D.) and that the preserved Greek text is the Beza 1589 edition. I can't absolutely prove these, but the cumulative evidence leans heavily in that direction and I KNOW that the United Bible Society/Nestle-Aland/Westcott-Hort Greek text and Leningrad Hebrew are NOT the preserved text. This is provable as seen in these two chapters (which are really a brief summary of a complex subject). One point of several that the reader might want to consider is that God did not necessarily promise to preserve his Words in ONE book. Each of the 66 books of the Bible stands on its own. If God chose to preserve each one separately then that is His prerogative. Nevertheless, I believe by faith that He preserved the texts in a group as stated above. The Bible says that faith is "the <u>evidence</u> of things not seen." In other words, there is real evidence to support what I am saying, but we cannot see everything that is necessary to prove it in the absolute sense. Furthermore, the Bible states that "without faith it is impossible to please him" (God). This is not a blind faith, but a faith backed by the evidence.

Many scholars claim that no theology is affected by using the wrong Bible, but this has been documented to be untrue by Dr. Jack Moorman, who identified 356 theologically important problems with using the wrong Greek text (not counting the Hebrew text).[16] There are doctrinal errors with regard to the Trinity, ecclesiology, angelology, Satanology, Bibliology, Eschatology, Soteriology, and Christology.[17]

Let's briefly examine three examples of the 356 differences, Mark 16:9-20, Luke 2:33, and 1 John 5:7-8.

The Last 12 Verses of Mark

Mark 16:9-20 is completely missing in *Codex Vaticanus* and *Codex Sinaiticus*. However, it is in the Greek *Textus Receptus*. The modern English translations either do not include this passage or there is a footnote that basically states that the passage in question is not found in the earliest and best manuscripts. This passage has multiple doctrinally important citations as well as theologically important citations and it should be included as true Scripture. The great commission is given in this passage. Jesus' resurrection is attested to in this passage. There is an acknowledgement of Jesus' power over demons (devils). It attests to his appearances after His resurrection. It attests to the ability of the believers to cast out devils through the power of Jesus Christ. It witnesses to Jesus' ascension. Without the passage the book ends oddly. In other words, the sense is scrambled without the passage. By removing the passage, the Roman Catholic false doctrines are legitimized. Interestingly, both the *Codex Vaticanus* and *Codex Sinaiticus* have the exact amount of space left blank on their parchment that Mark 16:9-20 would fit into before beginning the next book in the manuscript. Clearly the Vatican had the passage removed to support their erroneous thinking.

Joseph, Jesus' Adoptive Father

In the next example, the King James Bible translation of Luke 2:33 states,

> *And Joseph and his mother marvelled at those things which were spoken of him.*

'Joseph' is changed to 'his father' in Greek in the false Greek text.[18] This is a blatant attempt by the critics to deny the virgin birth of Christ. They attempt to name Joseph as Jesus' literal father, when in fact he was not. The change is in both false codices (*Vaticanus* and *Sinaiticus*). In modern English translations it is usually translated "And the child's father...," which is clearly incorrect.

Comma Johanneum

In our third example, 1 John 5:7-8 states,

> *For there are three that bear record in heaven, the Father, the Word, and the Holy Ghost: and these three are one. And there are three that bear witness in earth, the Spirit, and the water, and the blood: and these three agree in one.*

Codex Vaticanus and *Codex Sinaiticus* remove the middle portion of the passage to state it as (English translation),

> There are three that bear record, the spirit and the water and the blood; and these three agree.

By removing this section of the passage, the only passage in the Bible that clearly delineates the doctrine of the Trinity, the critics have succeeded in allowing for questioning the truth of the tripartite

Godhead. Yet, the passage clearly belongs for at least six reasons.

1. **Supporting Roots**: The passage is cited by ancient writers such as Tertullian (ca. 200 A.D.), Cyprian (200-258 A.D.),[19] and Priscillian (ca. 350 A.D.), and it is in all the Old Latin manuscripts. It is in 98% of the Latin Vulgate editions. It dominates the cursives.

2. **Greek Witnesses**: It is cited in ancient Greek manuscripts (numbers 61, 88, 221, 629, 429, 635, 636, 918, and 2382). Many modern scholars claim that the passage is found nowhere in ancient Greek, but that is simply not true.

3. **Grammar**: The context of the passage requires it; otherwise the grammar would be foul. The gender and number in the Greek DO NOT agree without the passage from the *Textus Receptus* included. God does not make grammar errors, so *Codex Sinaiticus* and *Codex Vaticanus* are again proven wrong.

4. **Key Sources Unregenerate**: This was discussed the previous chapter and is explained in more detail in the appendix.

5. **Historic Church**: There is good evidence that 1 John 5:7-8 (*Textus Receptus* version) was in the Scripture manuscripts that have been used by the majority of true believers over the last 1,900+ years. It was even in the Bible used by Roman Catholics up until the 19th century. No true believers have EVER questioned the authenticity of the text until the last century.

6. **Testification of Scripture**: God said in His Word that He would preserve His Word and Words forever and ever. So, ripping a passage

out of the critics false Bible in the 1800s does not change the fact that it belongs there and, in fact, it remains there in the *Textus Receptus* and in the King James Authorized Bible.

I could go through 353 more examples of theological error that are brought to bear by using the wrong Bible, but the purpose of these two chapters is to briefly outline the problems with the bad Greek text that is the source text behind the English Standard Version, the New International Version, the New American Standard Version, the New World Version, the New King James Version (heavy influence upon), the Holman Christian Standard Version, and almost every other version in use today in English except the King James Bible. If the diligent reader wishes to examine these issues further, I encourage him/her to read some of the books listed in the Bibliography to this book and compare what each author claims with regard to what the Bible says.

These chapters have been necessary because there are so many people who are deceived by this important issue. May God bless your journey, dear reader, as you continue to ferret out absolute truth. Pray for wisdom, which God is happy to grant to the sincere believer.

> *If any of you lack wisdom, let him ask of God, that giveth to all men liberally, and upbraideth not; and it shall be given him.* James 1:5

Endnotes

1. Marlowe, Michael; Bible Research: Internet Resources for Students of Scripture, http://www.bible-researcher.com/rules.html (accessed September 26, 2016).

2. Ibid.

3. *Bridge to Babylon*, directed by Christian Pinto, Adullam Films, Adullamfilms.com, AF Publishing, Mount Juliet, TN.

4. Cooper, William; *The Forging of Codex Sinaiticus* (England, Kindle edition, 2016), Kindle locations 122-250.

5. Ibid., Kindle locations 185-336.

6. Ibid., Kindle locations 289-311.

7. Ibid., Kindle locations 360-427.

8. Jones, Floyd Nolen; *The Septuagint: A Critical Analysis* (The Woodlands, TX: KingsWord Press, 2000), 21.

9. Cooper, William, *The Forging of Codex Sinaiticus* (England, Kindle edition, 2016), Kindle Locations 748-751.

10. Ibid., Kindle Locations 842-845.

11. Ibid.

12. Ibid.

13. Ibid., 1392-1473.

14. Ibid., Kindle locations 1719-1889.

15. Ibid., Kindle Locations 1746-1751.

16. Moorman, Jack; *Early Manuscripts, Church Fathers, and the Authorized Version* (Collingswood, NJ: The Bible for Today Press, 2005), Preface.

17. Waite, D.A.; *Defending the King James Bible* (Collingswood, NJ: The Bible for Today Press, 2006), 131-183.

18. Moorman, Jack; *8,000 Differences Between the N.T. Greek Words of the King James Bible and the Modern Versions* (Collingswood, NJ: The Bible for Today Press and The Dean Burgon Society (joint printing), 2006), 130.

19. Jack Moorman, *Early Manuscripts, Church Fathers, and the Authorized Version* (Collingswood, NJ: The Bible for Today Press, 2005), 429.

CHAPTER 6

ADDING UP THE YEARS

Having built a case for the trustworthiness of an inerrant, infallible, and authoritative Scripture, and for which translated Bible in English should be used for this purpose, and for which Greek and Hebrew texts should be referred to for absolute truth, the time has come to add up the years from creation to the present time using the Scripture alone as the source. In subsequent chapters, I'll share more information from sources outside the Bible including geochronological studies, statistical data, empirical data, and historical records that all support the conclusion obtained from the purest source—the Bible. The cumulative effect of the data makes it very, very difficult for even the most logical rationalist to deny the truth herein.

Jesus defined the beginning of the human world in His teachings in several passages of Scripture, including:

> *And he answered and said unto them, Have ye not read, that he which made them at the beginning made them male and female...* Matthew 19:4

> *But from the beginning of the creation God made them male and female.* Mark 10:6

Our Lord Jesus points to the fact that man and woman were created on the sixth day and that first week of creation was the beginning of time—the very first period of the existence of the universe and earth and of the things that filled the earth and the heavens. Christ further clarifies in John 8:44 (referring to the devil):

> *He was a murderer from the beginning, and*

> *abode not in the truth, because there is no truth in him. When he speaketh a lie, he speaketh of his own: for he is a liar, and the father of it.*

The Apostle John weighs in as well:

> *...for the devil sinneth from the beginning.*
> 1 John 3:8

Both of these passages make it clear that Satan was present at the start of time and that he was a sinner from the earliest days. The writer of Hebrews makes it obvious that the Lord created everything *at the beginning* of time:

> *And, Thou, Lord, in the beginning hast laid the foundation of the earth; and the heavens are the works of thine hands:* Hebrews 1:10

And Jesus elucidates the fact that there was a time at the very beginning when man was not sinful (before the fall):

> *For in those days shall be affliction, such as was not from the beginning of the creation which God created unto this time, neither shall be.* Mark 13:19

This means that in the beginning, everything was very good—that is before the fall of man. In fact, that is what the Bible tells us in Genesis 1:31:

> *And God saw every thing that he had made, and, behold, it was very good.*

These passages also tell us that the beginning was a defined point in time as related to mankind. Anything before that was timeless (eternal). The goal here is to try to determine when time began and how long mankind, the universe, and the planet earth have been around.

The first six days can be accounted for in Genesis

1:1-31. These were days that were literal (not long ages) and were good by God's definition of good (not man's definition). We can know this because God defined each day by an evening and morning.

The First Six Days

The first week of time can be summed up by the following table:

Day One	Genesis 1:1-5	Heavens & earth created, waters, light, division of light from dark
Day Two	Genesis 1:6-8	Firmament, division of the waters by the firmament
Day Three	Genesis 1:9-13	Division of water from dry land, trees, flowers, and all general flora created
Day Four	Genesis 1:14-19	Sun, moon, and stars created
Day Five	Genesis 1:20-23	Swimming and flying creatures created
Day Six	Genesis 1:24-31	Land animals, man and woman created

Since Jesus so kindly clarified that the beginning involved the creation of man and woman (Matthew 19:4, Mark 10:6), we now know that this really is the first week of time and that history was beginning to be made (time had started). Additionally, we can know that no sin had yet entered into the world, which means that millions of years of death, suffering, and pain could not have been occurring before man was created (as some would suppose).

The First Thousand Years

After going through the explanation in chapters two and three regarding the inerrancy, veracity, and authority of Scripture, it is easy to see that we can trust our source, the Bible, for information that might lead us to a calculation from the beginning of time, regarding the age of the earth. In Chapter Five of Genesis, there is a genealogical list of patriarchs from the first man, Adam, who was created on day six, at the beginning, to Noah of the global flood and ark fame:

> *And* ***Adam lived an hundred and thirty years, and begat a son in his own likeness, and after his image; and called his name Seth****: And the days of Adam after he had begotten Seth were eight hundred years: and he begat sons and daughters: And all the days that Adam lived were nine hundred and thirty years: and he died. And* ***Seth lived an hundred and five years, and begat Enos****: And Seth lived after he begat Enos eight hundred and seven years, and begat sons and daughters: And all the days of Seth were nine hundred and twelve years: and he died. And* ***Enos lived ninety years, and begat Cainan****: And Enos lived after he begat Cainan eight hundred and fifteen years, and begat sons and daughters: And all the days of Enos were nine*

hundred and five years: and he died. And ***Cainan lived seventy years and begat Mahalaleel****: And Cainan lived after he begat Mahalaleel eight hundred and forty years, and begat sons and daughters: And all the days of Cainan were nine hundred and ten years: and he died. And* ***Mahalaleel lived sixty and five years, and begat Jared****: And Mahalaleel lived after he begat Jared eight hundred and thirty years, and begat sons and daughters: And all the days of Mahalaleel were eight hundred ninety and five years: and he died. And* ***Jared lived an hundred sixty and two years, and he begat Enoch****: And Jared lived after he begat Enoch eight hundred years, and begat sons and daughters: And all the days of Jared were nine hundred sixty and two years: and he died. And* ***Enoch lived sixty and five years, and begat Methuselah****: And Enoch walked with God after he begat Methuselah three hundred years, and begat sons and daughters: And all the days of Enoch were three hundred sixty and five years: And Enoch walked with God: and he was not; for God took him. And* ***Methuselah lived an hundred eighty and seven years, and begat Lamech****. And Methuselah lived after he begat Lamech seven hundred eighty and two years, and begat sons and daughters: And all the days of Methuselah were nine hundred sixty and nine years: and he died. And* ***Lamech lived an hundred eighty and two years, and begat a son: And he called his name Noah****, saying, This same shall comfort us concerning our work and toil of our hands, because of the ground which the Lord hath cursed. And Lamech lived after he begat Noah five hundred ninety and five years, and begat sons and daughters: And all the days of Lamech were seven hundred seventy and*

> *seven years: and he died. And Noah was five hundred years old: and Noah begat Shem, Ham, and Japheth. Genesis 5:3-31* [bold by author]

Adding up the ages to the birth of each son by each father we arrive at:

> Adam(130) + Seth(105) + Enos(90) + Cainan(70) + Mahalaleel(65) + Jared(162) + Enoch(65) + Methuselah(187) + Lamech(182 years to the birth of Noah) = 1,056 years

It is important to note that some have disputed this account on the basis that the genealogy in 1 Chronicles is slightly different because of different spellings. However, this has been expertly refuted by Robert Dick Wilson.[1] It has also been suggested that sometimes genealogies in the Bible are listed as the grandfather representing the father in a lineage (which is sometimes true). However, the names are not particularly relevant to this calculation except to denote the order of the births. Genesis Chapter Five gives the years, which is what we are focusing on in this chapter, and they are without error.

A minor problem arises in determining the time of year each child was born. For example, we do not know whether Mahalaleel was born in January, June, December, or one of the other nine months. Additionally, we do not know what month his son Jared was born. We only know that it was sometime in the 65th year of Mahalaleel's life. Therefore, we must consider the possibility that 11 months and 29 days (359/360ths of a year) might have to be added to the birth year of each son within each man's father's life in the lineage.[2] Further, we cannot know for certain whether the term 'begat' which is used over and over again in the genealogical record of Genesis Chapter Five means 'time of conception' or 'time of the baby taking his first breath.'

So, at this point in the calculation there are 1,056 years that have passed since the beginning plus an error bar up to 17 years (more details on this issue are provided in the next section and explained in a chart), including the first six days of creation.

The Next Nine Hundred Years

Picking up after the birth of Lamech's son, Noah, we learn that Noah was 600 years old when the flood covered the entire earth,

> *And Noah was six hundred years old when the flood of waters was upon the earth.* Genesis 7:6

From Genesis 5:31 as cited in the previous section, we know that Noah had three sons: Shem, Ham and Japheth. His oldest son, Shem, fathered his son, Arphaxad, two years after the flood:

> *These are the generations of Shem: Shem was an hundred years old, and begat Arphaxad two years after the flood:* Genesis 11:10

So, at this point it is necessary to add two years (a third year might need to be added, because the flood period lasted a bit over a year and we do not know whether the writer meant that Arphaxad's being begat was referring to the beginning of the flood, the end of the flood (40 days), or to the end of the flood period (377 days)) to the chronology and begin again calculating through the genealogies in Genesis chapter 11:

> *And Arphaxad lived five and thirty years,*

and begat Salah: Genesis 11:12

And Salah lived thirty years, and begat Eber: Genesis 11:14

And Eber lived four and thirty years, and begat Peleg: Genesis 11:16

And Peleg lived thirty years, and begat Reu: Genesis 11:18

And Reu lived two and thirty years, and begat Serug: Genesis 11:20

And Serug lived thirty years, and begat Nahor: Genesis 11:22

And Nahor lived nine and twenty years, and begat Terah: Genesis 11:24

And Terah lived seventy years, and begat Abram, Nahor, and Haran. Genesis 11:26

Adding up the series:

Noah(600 years to flood) + Shem(2 years to Arphaxad's birth) + Arphaxad(35) + Salah(30) + Eber(34) + Peleg(30) + Reu(32) + Serug(30) + Nahor(29) + Terah(70 years to the birth of Abram) = 892 years

Next, as stated earlier, it is necessary to take into account the fact that we do not know the precise birth dates of these patriarchs. Without getting too complicated, we will consider that each of the above years must be true within two years (nine months for gestation and up to 359/360th's of a year for births which didn't occur on the father's birthday, and then rounded up), based on the fact that we do not know the precise month in which they were born. Thus, it can be seen in Chart 'A', derived thanks to Dr. James J. S. Johnson, Institute for Creation Research (2008)[3], that the minimum number of years from Adam to Abram is 1,948 and the maximum number of years from Adam to Abram is 1,985. We could add to that the first five days of the creation week (Adam was created on the sixth day), but that only adds less than 1/52 of a year to the total; for the purposes of this work, it is my intent to round numbers to keep it from getting excessively complicated.

There is one issue that needs to be addressed at this point, however, because these passages give us additional information:

> *So Abram departed, as the LORD had spoken unto him; and Lot went with him: and Abram was seventy and five years old when he departed out of Haran.* Genesis 12:4

> *And the days of Terah were two hundred and five years: and Terah died in Haran.* Genesis 11:32

> *Then came he out of the land of the Chaldaeans, and dwelt in Charran* [same as Haran]*: and from thence, when his father* [presumably referring to Terah, Abram's father,

> but maybe not as explained further on] *was dead, he removed him into this land, wherein ye now dwell.* Acts 7:4

Considering these passages together, one question might be: was Abram born in Terah's 70th year and perhaps as a triplet as Genesis 11:26 possibly implies.

> *And Terah lived seventy years, and begat Abram, Nahor, and Haran.*

Or was Abram 75 years old when Terah died at age 205 (205 minus 75 = 130) while living in Haran, since Acts 7:4 may seem to imply that Abraham did not leave Haran until Terah was dead. Also, Genesis 11:32 might seem to imply that Abram was actually born to Terah when Terah was 130 years old; it might be even be possible that Abram was born when Terah was 130 years old, because the Hebrew can be translated to mean that Terah began to have children at age 70.[4] This would mean that Terah's firstborn was not Abram, but maybe Haran.[5] Presumably, by this interpretation, Abram was listed first in the list of sons since he is the focus of the story in this section of the Bible, but normally that spot is reserved for the firstborn. So the years to Abram according to this interpretation are as follows: (5 days of creation before Adam rolled into other years as an insignificant part of the calculation) + 1056 (Adam to Noah's birth) + 892 years (Noah to Abram) + 60 (possible correction for Abram's birth year) = 2,008 plus (+) up to 37 years (the cumulative error bar so far) for not knowing the month of begetting each child or the month of the age of the father when the child was begat/minus (-) zero (see Chart 'A' for further understanding).

A second possibility and more logical interpretation is that Abram reburied his father.[6] The practice of reburial was not unknown in history. The case for this is well established in a scholarly paper by James J.S. Johnson.[7] This interpretation and the next leave no necessity for adding 60 years to the cumulative calculation at this point. It is important to note that in no way can any of these interpretations be justification for declaring that the Bible is errant and fallible. It is simply a case that we mere men have not yet figured out absolute answers within the confines of God's revealed Word. So the reader should not get carried away by believing that we somehow have a right to an absolute answer. That is not true, unless God chooses to reveal it to us.

A third possibility exists with regard to interpreting the Abram and Terah age issue, which is also very logical and fits the Biblical passages being studied here. This centers around the interpretation of Acts 7:4 which states (Stephen, the martyr, speaking of Abraham):

> *Then came he out of the land of the Chaldaeans, and dwelt in Charran* [same as Haran]*: and from thence, when his father was dead, he removed him into this land, wherein ye now dwell.*

This is supposed to prove (for some) that Abram was 75 years old when his own father, Terah, died, but the Scripture *does not specify* that it was Abram's own father who died. In fact, it quite possibly refers to Abram's patriarchal father, Noah, who died within at least two years of this date[8,9] and possibly exactly in this year. Perhaps, Noah lived in the Haran area and Abram spent some time with him and had some truths about the creation and the flood revealed to him at that time in his life. I cannot prove this absolutely, but I think there is a strong circumstantial case for it.

Moving on, the following calculation is derived without a 60-year adjustment:

(5 days of creation before Adam) + 1056 (Adam to Noah) +892 (Noah to Abram) =

1,948 years (+) up to 37 years (explained above)/(-) 0

Up to this point, the calculations are pretty much irrefutable except by bad logic or an assumption that the Bible is not inerrant. If one assumes that the entire Bible or even part of the Bible is inerrant, then one must take a position against what the Bible itself (God's Word) testifies on its own behalf, which is an absolutely untenable position.

Chart A[3]

The timeframe in years from Adam's creation to Abraham's birth, based on event-to-event timeframe "links" as recorded in Genesis					
Timeframe "Links"	**Bookend Events**	**Womb Time**	**Stated Years**	**Partial Year**	**Total Years**
1. Genesis 5:3	Adam is created / Adam begets Seth	n/a	130	≤ 1	≤ 131
2. Genesis 5:6	Seth is begotten / Seth begets Enosh	≤ 1	105	≤ 1	≤ 107
3. Genesis 5:9	Enosh is begotten / Enosh begets Cainan	≤ 1	90	≤ 1	≤ 92
4. Genesis 5:12	Cainan is begotten / C. begets Mahalaleel	≤ 1	70	≤ 1	≤ 72
5. Genesis 5:15	Mahalaleel is begotten/ M. begets Jared	≤ 1	65	≤ 1	≤ 67
6. Genesis 5:18	Jared is begotten / Jared begets Enoch	≤ 1	162	≤ 1	≤ 164
7. Genesis 5:21	Enoch is begotten / E. begets Methusaleh	≤ 1	65	≤ 1	≤ 67
8. Genesis 5:25	Methusaleh is begotten/ M. begets Lamech	≤ 1	187	≤ 1	≤ 189
9. Genesis 5:28-29	Lamech is begotten / Lamech begets Noah	≤ 1	182	≤ 1	≤ 184
10. Genesis 7:6	Noah is begotten / Flood hits	≤ 1	600	≤ 1	≤ 602
11. Genesis 11:10	Flood hits / Arphaxad is begotten	n/a	2	≤ 1	≤ 3
12. Genesis 11:12	Arphaxad is begotten / A. begets Shelah	≤ 1	35	≤ 1	≤ 37
13. Genesis 11:14	Shelah is begotten / Shelah begets Eber	≤ 1	30	≤ 1	≤ 32
14. Genesis 11:16	Eber is begotten / Eber begets Peleg	≤ 1	34	≤ 1	≤ 36
15. Genesis 11:18	Peleg is begotten / Peleg begets Reu	≤ 1	30	≤ 1	≤ 32
16. Genesis 11:20	Reu is begotten / Reu begets Serug	≤ 1	32	≤ 1	≤ 34
17. Genesis 11:22	Serug is begotten / Serug begets Nahor	≤ 1	30	≤ 1	≤ 32
18. Genesis 11:24	Nahor is begotten / Nahor begets Terah	≤ 1	29	≤ 1	≤ 31
19. Genesis 11:26	Terah is begotten / Abraham is born	≤ 1 + ≤ 1[2]	70	≤ 1	≤ 73
			Total: ≥ 1,948		Total: ≤ 1,985

Abraham to The Exodus

If the genealogies continue to be followed, we ultimately get trapped:

> *And Abraham was an hundred years old, when his son Isaac was born unto him.* Genesis 21:5

So that adds 100 years. Then the Bible tells us that Jacob was born to Isaac when he was 60 years old.

> *And after that came his brother out, and his hand took hold on Esau's heel; and his name was called Jacob: and Isaac was threescore years old when she bare them.* Genesis 25:26

At this point, a considerable number of assumptions need to be made in order to continue following the lineages, and a decision would need to be made regarding which of Jacob's 12 sons should be tracked. Perhaps, this could be done by tracking Levi through Moses, or Judah through Jesus, and then by cross-referencing it with someone else's lineage. The problem is that none of these lineages can be precisely calculated with confidence. Many of the birth years in the Bible are not given with the father's age at the time of birth and the error bars increase substantially as time passes because of the built-in assumptions in each successive generation. So, the best thing to do is to back-pedal to Abram and to locate the Biblical passages that are useful in tracing the historical chronology forward from that point.

Picking up with Genesis 12:4:

> *So Abram departed, as the LORD had spoken unto him; and Lot went with him: and Abram was seventy and five years old when he departed out of Haran.*

This puts the chronology at 2023 *Anno Mundi* (year of the world). If the reader agrees with adding 60 years for a later Abrahamic birth, then you should go with 2083. At this point, I will be sticking with the 2023 A.M. number, since I do not see the need for human manipulation to interpret the Bible to favor a position (the reader should note that I have dropped the 60 years from the error bar for the remaining calculations). Abram then entered Canaan as verified by Genesis 12:6:

> *And Abram passed through the land unto the place of Sichem, unto the plain of Moreh. And the Canaanite was then in the land.*

After that:

> *And Abram journeyed, going on still toward the south. And there was a famine in the land: and Abram went down into Egypt to sojourn there; for the famine was grievous in the land.*
> Genesis 12:9-10

Abram then returned to what would eventually become the land of Israel and then, many years later, his progeny ended up in Egypt after his great grandson, Joseph, became the governor under Pharaoh.

There are four key passages from Scripture to consider at this point in the calculations.

First, Exodus 12:40-41 tells us:

> *Now the sojourning of the children of Israel, who dwelt in Egypt, was four hundred and thirty years. And it came to pass at the end of the four hundred and thirty years, even the selfsame day it came to pass, that all the hosts of the Lord went out from the land of Egypt.*

An additional substantiation comes from:

> *And this I say, that the covenant, that was confirmed before of God in Christ, the law, which was four hundred and thirty years after, cannot disannul, that it should make the promise of none effect.* Galatians 3:17

Yet other passages seem to throw a wrench in the problem.

> *And he said unto Abram, Know of a surety that thy seed shall be a stranger in a land that is not theirs, and shall serve them; and they shall afflict them four hundred years; And also that nation, whom they shall serve, will I judge: and afterward shall they come out with great substance. And thou shalt go to thy fathers in peace; thou shalt be buried in a good old age. But in the fourth generation they shall come hither again…* Genesis 15:13-16

> *And God spake on this wise, That his seed should sojourn in a strange land; and that they should bring them into bondage, and entreat them evil four hundred years.* Acts 7:6

I don't think it is best to be dogmatic about the interpretation of Scripture when establishing precise dates between Abram and the Exodus because perhaps God did not want us to be able to calculate the age of the earth to the very day and hour as Ussher did in his chronology.[10] Nevertheless, I believe we can get reasonably close. With that in mind, I want to consider the 'bookends' from the range of possibilities in interpreting Scripture within this time frame.

With regard to the date for the Exodus, the 430 years may represent the period from Abram's first arrival in the land of Canaan to the Exodus of Moses' time. It could also represent the period from the establishment of God's covenant with Abram to the

Exodus. Some scholars think that the entire 430 years require the Israelites being in Egypt. While this is barely possible, it seems unlikely. The clause, "who dwelt in Egypt" from Exodus 12:40 being set off by parenthesis (in English) could be taken as a parenthetical clause that simply identifies the group that happened to end up in Egypt rather than the group that spent the entire 430 years in Egypt. Furthermore, with the additional information from Genesis 15 and Acts 7, Scripture seems to indicate that the 400 years was a subset of the 430 years.

If we start with Jacob's (Abram's grandson) entry into Egypt and meeting the Pharaoh, we can see that the time is limited no matter how you interpret it. When Jacob entered Egypt he was 130 years old:

> *And Jacob said unto Pharaoh, The days of the years of my pilgrimage are an hundred and thirty years: few and evil have the days of the years of my life been, and have not attained unto the days of the years of the life of my fathers in the days of their pilgrimage.* Genesis 47:9

One of Jacob's sons was Levi. We don't know how old Jacob was when Levi was born, but the chronology is limited by the years that are documented in the Bible from Jacob's time to Moses. Moses' father was Amram, who lived 137 years. Amram's father was Kohath, who lived 133 years. Kohath's father was Levi (one of the twelve brothers who travelled to Egypt during the time Joseph was running the operations of the country), who lived to be 137 years old. Moses lived 80 years to the time of his calling to confront Pharaoh and to 120 years total. When you add up these years 80+137+133+137 = 487 years and then subtract 57 years (average of 19 years for each man besides Moses, because we already know his age when he began his mission to lead the Israelites out of Egypt) to account for the unlikely idea that each man fathered a child in the absolute last years of his life, we arrive at 430 years, which works with the Biblical 430 years referred to here. Furthermore, Moses' mother, Jochebed, was Kohath's sister (Levi's daughter), which binds the timeline range very tightly within this period of years, because of this additional corroboration.

The idea of fathering a child late in life was not uncommon then and it even occurs in modern times. People lived longer then and they had a lot of children. At least one of Levi's brothers had more than four generations of children from himself to the Exodus (Joseph), but that is not relevant to the four generations cited here which is authenticated by Genesis 15:16.

Some readers may have difficulty wrapping their minds around this idea, so consider the following truth from modern history. Two of former President John Tyler's (1790-1862) grandsons are alive today. I am referring to his grandsons NOT his great grandsons. Tyler had a son named Lyon Gardiner Tyler in 1853 (late in President Tyler's life). Lyon lived to 1935. Harrison Ruffin Tyler was born to Lyon in 1928 (late in Lyon's life). Lyon also fathered Lyon Tyler, Jr. in 1924. Both of these men are alive today (last I checked). Yet their grandfather was born in the 1700s. Unusual? Yes! Reality? Yes!

Knowing that the maximum time from some unknown event to the Exodus is 430 years is helpful. Yet the question remains as to what that initial event was that started the 430 years. Was it the covenant, Abram's entry into Canaan or something else? Scholars disagree on this point, but everyone seems to agree that the 430 years ended at the Exodus.

For our purposes here, the beginning of the 430 years could have been when Levi first entered Egypt or perhaps it began 30 years before (justified by Genesis 15:13). This was the point (if it began with Levi) where Jacob was 130 years old at his meeting with Pharaoh. Jacob died 17 years later and Joseph died at age 110, or 54 years after his father passed away.[11] After Joseph's death, 64 years passed before the birth of Moses.[12] The length of the bondage was at least 80 years, since that is how old Moses was when the Exodus occurred.

> *And Moses was fourscore years old, and Aaron fourscore and three years old, when they spake unto Pharaoh.* Exodus 7:7

The period of bondage would probably not have exceeded 144 years if the following passage refers to the period after Joseph's death, since the Bible says the Israelites were treated well for awhile (presumably up to Joseph's death).

> *Now there arose up a new king over Egypt, which knew not Joseph. And he said unto his people, Behold, the people of the children of Israel are more and mightier than we: Come on, let us deal wisely with them; lest they multiply, and it come to pass, that, when there falleth out any war, they join also unto our enemies, and fight against us, and so get them up out of the land. Therefore they did set over them taskmasters to afflict them with their burdens. And they built for Pharaoh treasure cities, Pithom and Raamses. But the more they afflicted them, the more they multiplied and grew. And they were grieved because of the children of Israel. And the Egyptians made the children of Israel to serve with rigour: And they made their lives bitter with hard bondage, in morter, and in brick, and in all manner of*

> *service in the field: all their service, wherein they made them serve, was with rigour.* Exodus 1:8-14

It could also be true that another Pharaoh came into power while Joseph was still living and didn't know anything about him or what he had done for Egypt. If this is the case, then the bondage could have lasted more than 144 years. At any rate, the total numbers add up to 430, one way or another.

So, the only apparent difficulties with adding the 430 years to the timeline is to determine the starting point. Was it Abraham's entering Canaan (or Levi's entering Egypt) and how does the 400 years mentioned in Genesis 15:13 fit in.

> *And he said unto Abram, Know of a surety that thy seed shall be a stranger in a land that is not theirs, and shall serve them; and they shall afflict them four hundred years.*

The 400 years in this passage, which does not agree with the 430 years in Exodus 12:40 and Galatians 3:17, can be justified by understanding what the verse does not say. It does not say that the Israelites would be in bondage for 400 full years. In fact, it could be understood that they were only in Egypt for 215 years, which agrees with other passages in Scripture.[13] The Hebrew word עָנָה (*anah*) which is translated 'afflict' in Genesis 15:13 also means 'to be troubled,' or 'to be humbled.' It is not required to have anything to do with bondage (although it could be associated with bondage). According to Young's Concordance, the word *anah* is translated both ways (troubled or humbled) in other passages in the Old Testament.

So, the passage can be (and almost certainly should be) understood to mean that the 400 years is a part of the 430 years. Another remote possibility is that the number was rounded by the writer of Genesis 15:13. Either way, it is not particularly important to this calculation as long as it is accepted that the 400 years is part of the 430 years.

If we calculate the end of the affliction as being at the time of the Exodus, then the beginning of the 400 years may have been around Isaac's fifth birthday, which would have been around the time of his weaning and the time he was first mocked by Ishmael[14] in Genesis 21:8-10.

> *And the child grew, and was weaned: and Abraham made a great feast the same day that Isaac was weaned. And Sarah saw the son of Hagar the Egyptian, which she had born unto Abraham, mocking. Wherefore she said unto Abraham, Cast out this bondwoman and her son: for the son of this bondwoman shall not be heir with my son, even with Isaac.* Genesis 21:8-10

So, it is possible and even likely that this was the designated beginning of the affliction of the children of Abram.[15] Also note Jacob's statement that he had lived a life of trouble in Genesis 47:9:

> *And Jacob said unto Pharaoh, The days of the years of my pilgrimage are an hundred and thirty years: few and evil have the days of the years of my life been, and have not attained unto the days of the years of the life of my fathers in the days of their pilgrimage.*

The alternative explanation for the 430 years would add another 215 years to the overall time line. There are a variety of reasons why I do not think that this position is tenable, but nevertheless, for argument's sake, the reader could add another 215 years to the error bar on the ever-increasing time line (on the plus side). For this work, I will not be adding the additional years to the error bar.

The Exodus to the Destruction of Jerusalem

The period from the Israelites departure from Egypt to the razing of Jerusalem by Nebuchadnezzar's Babylonian army is perhaps the most complex area we will examine.

1 Kings 6:1 states:

> *And it came to pass in the four hundred and eightieth year after the children of Israel were come out of the land of Egypt, in the fourth year of Solomon's reign over Israel, in the month Zif, which is the second month, that he began to build the house of the LORD.*

Yet, Acts 13:18-22a seems to disagree by quite a bit:

> *And about the time of forty years suffered he their manners in the wilderness. And when he had destroyed seven nations in the land of Chanaan* [Canaan], *he divided their land to them by lot. And after that he gave unto them judges about the space of four hundred and fifty years, until Samuel the prophet. And afterward they desired a king: and God gave unto them Saul the son of Cis, a man of the tribe of Benjamin, by the space of forty years. And when he had removed him, he raised up unto them David to be their king.*

This disagreement is especially difficult since the second passage only brings us up to King David's day and not all the way to the fourth year of Solomon's reign, which was still years away. In essence, there is a seeming difference of 131 years between the two passages from the Exodus to the beginning of the construction of the temple.[16]

The First Method

If we follow 1 Kings 6:1 line of thinking, this means 479 years plus a few days (the second month of the 480th year was when the work began) after the Israelites left Egypt, the temple construction began in earnest. The next relevant passages to the chronology are:

> *And the time that Solomon reigned in Jerusalem over all Israel was forty years.* 1 Kings 11:42

> *In the fourth year was the foundation of the house of the LORD laid, in the month Zif: And in the eleventh year, in the month Bul, which is the eighth month, was the house finished throughout all the parts thereof, and according to all the fashion of it. So was he seven years in building it.* 1 Kings 6:37-38

These passages clarify when the temple work began within the reign of Solomon (his fourth year as King). The foundation was laid early (the second month) in the fourth year of Solomon's reign. This means he had been king for three years up to this point. So, we subtract 37 years from his 40-year reign to arrive at the date in which the temple work began. This also means that 37 years is added to the chronology to arrive at the beginning of the split kingdom, which occurred after Solomon's death.

So, to recap:

1,948 years (Beginnings to Abram's birth) + 75 (Age of Abram when he departed Haran for Canaan) + 430 (Abram's entry into Canaan to the Exodus) + 479 (Exodus to Temple start) + 37 (remainder of Solomon's reign after temple start) = **2,969 years** and an error bar of +41 years of possible correction/ minus zero

Counting the years from the division of the kingdom after Solomon's death to the destruction of his temple adds up to 389 complete years. The destruction of the temple came in the 390th year, as supported by:

> *Lie thou also upon thy left side, and lay the iniquity of the house of Israel upon it: according to the number of the days that thou shalt lie upon it thou shalt bear their iniquity. For I have laid upon thee the years of their iniquity, according to the number of the days, three hundred and ninety days: so shalt thou bear the iniquity of the house of Israel. And when thou hast accomplished them, lie again on thy right side, and thou shalt bear the iniquity of the house of Judah forty days: I have appointed thee each day for a year.* Ezekiel 4:4-6

The days cited in this passage from Scripture are 390. The Lord also explains that each day represents a year.

I am grateful to Dr. Floyd Nolen Jones for his detailed analysis of the era of the split kingdoms in his book, *The Chronology of the Old Testament*. He explains in great detail how the Northern Kingdom and the Southern Kingdom used different dating methods to state when kings began and ended their reigns. He also correlated the data from both kingdoms to prove that there are 390 years between the end of Solomon's reign and the destruction of the temple. This interpretation is corroborated by other reliable sources.[17,18,19,20]

Adding 389 years to the last recap we have:

2,969 years + 389 years = 3,358 years after creation to the destruction of the temple in Jerusalem.

A Different View (probably the correct view)

If we follow the Acts 13:18-22a timeline and/or add up the years separately as follows, we end up with 611 years from the Exodus to the beginning of the temple building project:

Time spent in the wilderness	40 years
Time to conquer and divide the Promised Land	7 years
Acts 13:18-20 (until Samuel)	450 years
Up to Samuel's victory at Mizpeh	20 years
Up to King Saul's reign	10 years
King Saul's reign	40 years
King David's reign	40 years
Four years into Solomon's reign	4 years
Total	611 years[21]

To justify this view, we must examine each section. **First**, the time the Israelites spent in the wilderness after the Exodus is cited in numerous places in Scripture including:

> *For the children of Israel walked forty years in the wilderness, till all the people that were men of war, which came out of Egypt, were consumed, because they obeyed not the voice of the* L*ORD.* Joshua 5:6

The **second section** is proven out by Joshua 14:8,10, which states:

> *Forty years old was I when Moses the*

> *servant of the LORD sent me from Kadeshbarnea to espy out the land; and I brought him word again as it was in mine heart.*
>
> *And now, behold, the LORD hath kept me alive, as he said, these forty and five years, even since the LORD spake this word unto Moses, while the children of Israel wandered in the wilderness: and now, lo, I am this day fourscore and five years old.*

This means that 45 years had passed since Joshua had been sent out to spy on the land of Canaan. Yet, they were already two years into their wandering in the wilderness at that point. This is proven by Deuteronomy 2:14, which states:

> *And the space in which we came from Kadeshbarnea, until we were come over the brook Zered, was thirty and eight years; until all the generation of the men of war were wasted out from among the host, as the LORD sware unto them.*

So, 45 years (Joshua's age at the time he was sent to spy out the land) minus 38 years (remaining time spent wandering in the wilderness) equals seven years.

The **third section** is the period of the judges up until Samuel became Israel's leader. This is the 450 years referred to in Acts 13. This is a period of major contention between scholars (even conservative ones). Yet, because God is not the author of confusion (1 Corinthians 14:33), I am going to take the position that the judges did not overlap their periods of leadership and that we may add them up with the periods of rest that are cited in Scripture to reach a conclusion. This next chart lays out the years with the Judges names.

Table A[23]

Years of Oppression	Years of Rest	Judge
8	40	Othniel
18	80	Ehud, Shamgar
20	40	Deborah, Barak
7	40	Gideon
3		Abimelech
23		Tolah
22		Jair
18	6	Jephthah
7		Ibzan
10		Elon
8		Abdon
40		Samson
40		Eli

If the years are added together a number of 430 is derived. This leaves us 20 years short of the number from Acts 13. This is likely because there were 20 years between the conquering and dividing of the Promised Land and the first eight years of oppression. It could also be partly because there might have been some short rests (perhaps a few months in each case) between the judges who do not have rest credited to their time. Lastly, Luke uses the discriminator "about" in Acts 13:20 when quoting Paul:

> *about the space of four hundred and fifty years, until Samuel the prophet.*

I do not think that the term "about" would justify being 20 years off, but it might come into play with the other possibilities considered.

The **fourth section** is at least 20 years for the period from Eli's judgeship up to Samuel's victory at Mizpeh. This is obtained from 1 Samuel 7:2,

> *And it came to pass, while the ark abode in Kirjathjearim, that the time was long; for it was twenty years: and all the house of Israel lamented after the LORD.*

This was the time period at the end of which Eli died at age 98 (1 Samuel 4:15-18), and the Israelites lost the Ark of the Covenant to the Philistines and then regained it after the Philistines sent it back in a cart pulled by two young milk cows.

The **fifth section** from Table A covers the period from the victory at Mizpeh to Saul's reign. This is not a number named in Scripture, but must be calculated from the 480 years mentioned in 1 Kings 6:1, which are really part of the 611 years.[23] Without the ten years, we would end up with 470 years, which does not work. We will see how the totals add up in the end.

The **sixth section** is the length of Saul's reign, which was 40 years and is proven out by Acts 13:21.

The **seventh section** is the length of King David's reign and it was also 40 years long. This is supported by,

> *David was thirty years old when he began to reign, and he reigned forty years.*

The **last section** takes us to the beginning of the building of the temple in Jerusalem in King Solomon's day, which was four years into his reign as supported by 1 Kings 6:1:

> *And it came to pass in the four hundred and eightieth year after the children of Israel were come out of the land of Egypt, in the fourth year of Solomon's reign over Israel, in the month Zif, which is the second month, that he began to build the house of the LORD.*

This section explained how the 611 years is derived. The question remains: how can we explain the 480 years as being part of the 611 years?

Justifying the 480 Years as a Subset of the 611 Years

The reason that 611 years makes more sense than 480 years as a total over this period of time is that it is impossible to cram all of the reigns and events of the period in question into 480 years. Many Bible believers have tried and many have made very scholarly arguments for their claims, but in the end there are always several major problems that remain to be resolved. Explaining all of those subsets of problems is not the purpose of this work, since it would lengthen it by many, many pages. This work is to share a reasonable explanation for calculating the age of the earth using the Bible as a primary source and then backing it up with scientific data from extrabiblical sources. For that reason, not every part of these calculations is explained in detail and not every counterargument is rebutted. I have listed my source material in the bibliography, so that the diligent reader may continue his journey to study and learn about these things, if he is predisposed to do so.

Thanks to the marvelous work of Dr. Jack Moorman and Edward Denny, an excellent explanation is available for the 480 years being part of the 611 years.[24] The 131-year difference is explained as the years that the Israelites were out of fellowship with the LORD. If the reader will turn back to Table A, he will see that the years of oppression are exactly equal to 131 years. These are the years that men and women did whatever they wanted to do.

> *In those days there was no king in Israel: every man did that which was right in his own eyes. Judges 21:25*

Edward Denny suggested that the 480 years are not necessarily actual years, but may be thought of as *redemption years*.[25] When added to the seven years it took to build the temple and possibly three more years to furnish and decorate the temple,[26] one arrives at the amazing number of 490 years. Why is this number so amazing? Simply put,

> *And thou shalt number seven sabbaths of years unto thee, seven times seven years; and the space of the seven sabbaths of years shall be unto thee forty and nine years. Then shalt thou cause the trumpet of the jubile to sound on the tenth day of the seventh month, in the day of atonement shall ye make the trumpet sound throughout all your land.* Leviticus 25:8-9

Note that 49 years of Sabbaths (days of worship or rest) are to be adhered to before Jubilee (time of atonement) in the fiftieth year. This is similar to the 490 years (70 x 7 is the number of time the LORD requires for forgiveness according to Matthew 18:22) and the temple was dedicated in the seventh month (possibly the tenth day), which correlates with the above passage from Leviticus. After this, the people enjoyed a special time of fellowship with GOD and a period of unprecedented peace and prosperity. A coincidence? I don't think so.

So, the redemption years needed to be accounted for before the temple could be dedicated in order to agree with God's perfect math for such things. With God's redemption time, the Israelites were brought to a point of being divinely complete.[27]

Denny proposes ten Jubilee cycles of 490 years each throughout history.[28] He wrote that we must consider actual time AND redemption time together in order to fully understand how God's timing works.[29]

So, taking the 3,358 years calculated from the previous section to the destruction of Jerusalem and adding 131 years to account for the actual years that passed (480+131=611) we end up with:

3,489 years from creation to the destruction of Jerusalem

Destruction of the Temple to Christ

The final piece of the puzzle is calculated by first adding 70 years to the time of the destruction of the temple based on Jeremiah 25:11:

> *And this whole land shall be a desolation, and an astonishment; and these nations shall serve the king of Babylon seventy years.*

Then, after the 70 years was completed, Cyrus issued a decree to rebuild Jerusalem,

> *That saith of Cyrus, He is my shepherd, and shall perform all my pleasure: even saying to Jerusalem, Thou shalt be built; and to the temple, Thy foundation shall be laid.* Isaiah 44:28

This was the beginning point of the 70 weeks referred to by the prophet Daniel, which really refers to 70 x 7 years (each week being seven years) or 490 years.

> *Seventy weeks are determined upon thy people and upon thy holy city, to finish the transgression, and to make an end of sins, and to make reconciliation for iniquity, and to bring in everlasting righteousness, and to seal up the vision and prophecy, and to anoint the most Holy.* Daniel 9:24

At this point, we must look at the context to

understand the timing of events in order to overlay the correct number of years on the current calculation. Daniel was told in verses 25-27 of chapter nine:

> *25 Know therefore and understand, that from the going forth of the commandment to restore and to build Jerusalem unto the Messiah the Prince shall be seven weeks, and threescore and two weeks: the street shall be built again, and the wall, even in troublous times.*
>
> *26 And after threescore and two weeks shall Messiah be cut off, but not for himself: and the people of the prince that shall come shall destroy the city and the sanctuary; and the end thereof shall be with a flood, and unto the end of the war desolations are determined.*
>
> *27 And he shall confirm the covenant with many for one week: and in the midst of the week he shall cause the sacrifice and the oblation to cease, and for the overspreading of abominations he shall make it desolate, even until the consummation, and that determined shall be poured upon the desolate.*

In verse twenty-five, 69 of the 70 weeks are divided into 7 weeks (49 years) and 62 weeks (434 years) for a total of 69 weeks (483 years). Verse 25 tells us that it would take 49 years (7 weeks) to restore and [re]build Jerusalem from the time of the issuance of the commandment (Cyrus' decree). In verse 26, the Bible tells us that 434 years after that (62 weeks later), the Messiah would be cut off (crucified). After that various things will occur until the last week, which is believed to be equivalent to the seven years of tribulation referred to in the book of Revelation. At the end of the 70th week, Messiah (Jesus Christ our Lord) will return with an army and will pronounce judgment upon the world (the living and the dead).

While some will disagree with this method of calculating this period of time because they choose to lean on Ptolemy's (2nd century chronologist) calculations including his supposedly foolproof eclipse date that allegedly established the date of the destruction of Jerusalem to a specific date. The principal problem is that there is no known corroboration of Ptolemy's date for the eclipse and of his matching it to the same year as the date of Jerusalem's destruction.[30] Moreover, his assumptions do not bear up under scrutiny, because Persian kings end up out of place and misidentified. Also, people from the time would have had to live active lives for much, much longer than is even remotely reasonable if we use his dating system. This problem is brilliantly rebutted and explained in Dr. Jack Moorman's excellent work, *Bible Chronology, the Two Great Divides: A Defense of the Unbroken Biblical Chronology from Adam to Christ.*[31]

So, if we add up the years leading to the final calculation, we arrive at:

> 3,489 years + 70 years + 483 years = 4,042 years after creation (to Jesus' death and resurrection)

2,016 years have passed, since the *Anno Domini* (A.D.) time began, by the end of the year of finishing this writing. This brings me to the final calculation:

4,042 years + 2,016 - 33 years (to account for the period from the beginning of modern time (A.D.) to Messiah's resurrection =

6,025 years (age of the earth) +42 years/- 0

So the earth can't be any younger than 5,895 years (subtracting out the 131 years) or any older than 6,067 years as of December 31, 2016. That is to say, it cannot be 10,000 years old, or 25,000 years old or millions of years old or 4.5 billion years old, as some like to suppose. Furthermore, if one adds the 215 and the 60 years (explained previously) back into the error bar, it only loosens the age range to between 5,895 and 6,342, which is still very close to 6,000 years. However, I believe that the first view is the correct view and range. I believe Ussher, Moorman, and Jones were very close; it is even possible that they are correct. However, I believe that the absolute range for the age of the earth (and the universe) is between 5,895 to 6,342 years into the past.

If some parts of these calculations seem confusing, I encourage the reader to do some additional research by perusing some of the resources listed in the endnotes and the bibliography. Even if the reader disagrees with a section or sections of my calculations and chooses to add an additional 215 years and maybe even another 400 years, even by this there is no way to get up to a 7,000 year old earth, much less one that is 10,000 years old or billions of years old.

Endnotes

1. Wilson, Robert Dick; *A Scientific Investigation of the Old Testament* (Birmingham, AL: Solid Ground Christian Books, 1959), pp. 58-79.

2. Johnson, James J.S.; "How Young is the Earth? Applying Simple Math to Data in Genesis," *Acts & Facts*, (Dallas, TX: Institute for Creation Research, 2008), 37(10):4.

3. Ibid.

4. Lyons, Eric; (2004), "How Old was Terah when Abraham was Born?," 2003,

http://www.apologeticspress.org/apcontent.aspx?category=6&article=758 (accessed August 11, 2011).

5. Ussher, James; *The Annals of the World* (Green Forest, AR: Masterbooks, 2006), 22.

6. Johnson, James J.S.; "Comparing the Re-Burial of the Pagan King, "Gorm the Old" of Jutland, by his son, Harald Bluetooth, Viking king of Denmark, with The Re-Burial of the Pagan Idolater, Terah, formerly of Ur of the Chaldees, by his YaHWeH-worshipping son, Abraham, including observations of how Moses used *waw* consecutive verbs in Genesis 11-12," 2006 (Dallas, TX: Cross Timbers Institute, 2006)

7. Ibid.

8. Colin Heath, "The Death of Abraham's Father," http://www.bibleinsight.com/crn1p3.html (accessed August 14, 2011).

9. Ussher, James; *The Annals of the World* (Green Forest, AR: Masterbooks, 2006), 22.

10. Ibid., 17.

11. Jones, Floyd Nolen; *The Chronology of the Old Testament,* (Green Forest, AR: Masterbooks, 2009), 54. The 215 years is also supported by Josephus in his Antiquities of the Jews, II according to Jones (same page).

12. Ibid., 55.

13. Ibid., 56.

14. Ibid., 58.

15. Ibid., 49-60. For more complete details regarding the various arguments about the 430 versus the 400 year periods, Floyd Nolan Jones has written an excellent summation in this passage in his book, *The Chronology of the Old Testament.*

16. Moorman, J.A.; *Bible Chronology, the Two Great Divides: A Defense of the Unbroken Biblical Chronology from Adam to Christ* (Collingswood, NJ: The Bible for Today Press, 2010), 50.

17. Unger, Merrill F.; *The New Unger's Bible Handbook* (Chicago: Moody Publishers, 2005), 299.

18. Morris, Henry M.; *The New Defender's Study Bible* (Nashville, TN: World Publishing, 2006), 1180.

19. Walvoord, John F. and Roy B. Zuck; (1983), *The Bible Knowledge Commentary: Old Testament* (Colorado Springs, CO: David C. Cook, 1983), 1235-1236.

20. Packer, J.I., Merrill C. Tenney, and William White, Jr.; *The Bible Almanac* (Nashville,TN: Thomas Nelson, 1980), 61.

21. Moorman, J.A.; *Bible Chronology, the Two Great Divides: A Defense of the Unbroken Biblical Chronology from Adam to Christ* (Collingswood, NJ: The Bible for Today Press, 2010), 47.

22. Ibid., 50.

23. Ibid., 60.

24. Ibid., 15-67.

25. Ibid., 21.

26. Ibid., 62.

27. Ibid., 21.

28. Ibid.

29. Ibid.

30. Ibid., 15.

31. Ibid., 69-131.

CHAPTER 7

EXTRABIBLICAL GENEALOGICAL EVIDENCES

Up to this point, I've predominantly used the Bible to prove the age of the earth. Now I would like to present some extrabiblical material that I consider reliable. Floyd Nolen Jones predominantly used the Bible in his book, *The Chronology of the Old Testament* to reach his conclusion that the earth was created in 4004 B.C.[1] Archbishop James Ussher used the Bible and sources that no longer exist today to arrive at the same date, 4004 B.C., in his book, *The Annals of the World*.[2] This is almost within the sphere of my preferred dates cited in Chapter Six and easily within the possible range. The major difference of opinion between these two scholars and me is that I interpret Torah's age at Abram's birth differently than they do, as well as the period from the Exodus to the resurrection of Christ. However, I also grant the possibility that they may be exactly right on these points. In 1878, S.C. Adams published a Synchronological Chart, which adheres to the 4004 B.C. date.[3] Adams appears to have referred to Ussher's work and to the Bible in drawing his conclusions.

In 1978, John H. Walton published a book entitled *Chronological and Background Charts of the Old Testament* in which he used some extrabiblical sources to suppose an earth that was about 10,000 years aged.[4] Many great and scholarly men have endorsed the age of the earth being somewhere between 8,000 and billions of years. I think this is most likely due to the fact that they never really studied the issue in-depth, or perhaps, their ears were twisted to listening to liberal arguments resulting in a slight-togargantuan compromise. Some people realize that the earth is substantially younger than millions or billions of years old, but have difficulty counting the correct number of thousands of years for the age of the universe. Others have substantially compromised to become unwitting enablers of the devil's deception by believing in millions and billions of years of past earth history. This illustrates the danger of listening to those teachers referred to by Paul in his letter to Timothy:

> *For the time will come when they will not endure sound doctrine; but after their own lusts shall they heap to themselves teachers, having itching ears. And they shall turn away their ears from the truth, and shall be turned unto fables.* 2 Timothy 4:3-4

So, it is very, very important to know the truth, so that we will not easily be deceived. Why? Because as the Apostle Peter warns us:

> *Be sober, be vigilant; because your adversary the devil, as a roaring lion, walketh about, seeking whom he may devour.* 1 Peter 5:8

In 1995, Bill Cooper published *After the Flood*, a groundbreaking piece of modern scholarship that he researched for over 25 years. In his book, Cooper traced the lineages of several different nations' rulers by independent and unrelated sources, and which were not tied to the Bible at all. He traced the British kings, the Anglo-Saxon kings, the Danish kings, the Norwegian kings and the Irish Celtic kings back to Japheth, the son of Noah, by secular sources available to the public in libraries and through public archives in the British Isles and Europe.[5]

Cooper also cited several secular sources that declared the earth to be fewer than 7,212 years old, including:

Group or Individual	Believed earth's beginning traced to:
Saxons[6]	5200 B.C.
Irish	4000 B.C.
Joseph Scaliger[7]	4713 B.C.
Mayans	4769 B.C.[8]

None of these dates is within the Biblical error bar that I proved in the last chapter, but they are reasonably close. This chart demonstrates that some secular history clearly indicates an earth that is not over 7212 years aged (as of the end of 2012). Cooper does point out some flaws in their thinking, but the point is that these groups were generally on the right track. Had they had the Bible, they might have been able to tighten up their history and identify the corruptions within it. Today, since most really old literature is no longer in existence, it is impossible to determine where they went wrong.

Cooper also mentions some Chinese descendants in an appendix of his book, but doesn't cite dates. However, C. H. Kang and Ethel R. Nelson do mention dates in their book, *The Discovery of Genesis*. They state that the Chinese trace their roots to around 2500 B.C. which would have been around the time of the Tower of Babel,[9] when the nations were divided by languages.

Other sources 'punt' on the age of the earth. For example, Rose Publishing publishes a timeline title that states, "**More** than 6,000 years at a glance"[10] [my emphasis on the word 'more']. The way they handle their time line is to begin dating at Abraham and to leave the series of genealogies from Adam to Abraham for the reader to interpret (no dates are published). Perhaps this was done to seem inclusive to all types of interpretations (from thousands to billions). It certainly can't hurt their sales. But what about the truth?

Flood Legends

In support of the lineages spelled out in the previous section, there are a myriad of oral and written records of a favored family being saved from a great flood in almost every (if not all) ethnic history in the entire world.[11] Stories have been collected from over 200 sources from all over the world supporting a Noachic-like flood.[12] Each story varies a bit, because most do not, or did not, have a Bible (God's preserved Word) to keep them straight, but most know it happened, that it was global, and that it was God's punishment for the general wickedness that had permeated the earth up to that point.[13]

Many detractors like to say that the inconsistency of these stories should clue us in that they are mere myths. Yet, how is it that we get similar stories in nearly every language, being passed down for many, many generations, without there being some elements of truth therein? Secularists have no tenable explanation for this problem. Of course, creationists explain the universality of the story by way of the division of the languages during the building of the Tower of Babel in Genesis Chapter 11, which was after the global deluge of Noah's day. I've never read or heard an alternative explanation from any source that is not easily refutable.

The most likely explanation for the differences in the stories from culture to culture is the fact that history that is not written down soon after it occurred is likely to be distorted. This is especially true when it is passed down orally from generation to generation.

Moreover, when ethnic groups failed to acknowledge God as creator and sustainer of life, He withdrew His support and abandoned them to their wicked ways (Romans 1). This means that they also lost their real knowledge of God somewhere along the way.

There are many occasions in the past where the experts have been wrong when it came to interpreting historical writings. Take for example Homer's *Iliad* which was originally believed to be a fictional account, but subsequent archaeological discoveries have led modern academics to reconsider the strong possibility that the *Iliad* was non-fiction.[14] Another example is the not-so-ancient poem, *Beowolf*, which survives from an approximately 1,000-year-old copy of a tale from around the mid-eighth century.[15] I was taught in high school that Beowulf was a mythological Old-English poem, but it is actually based on a real historical character and real historical events according a chapter in the well-researched and eloquent book, *After the Flood*, by Bill Cooper.[16]

I merely mention these two simple examples as illustrations of the fact that history is often taught incorrectly by modernists. The point of this section is to further elucidate that there are sources outside the Bible which do point to the truth of the Scripture with regard to the Noachic Flood. I could spend a considerable number of words (tens of thousands perhaps) building the airtight case that real history fully supports the Bible, but hopefully the reader will find this short chapter to be sufficient for the purpose. Some readers may be interested in researching this topic in more depth and I do encourage you to do so, but before you do, read the next chapter on faith and logic. Bad interpretation of data leads to 'nowhere land.' Good thinking skills are required.

King Lists

Another source of extrabiblical information is in the various lists of ancient kings that have been inscribed on clay or stone for our modern edification. The Sumerian King List is one of the most well-known of these. This clay tablet is dated at approximately 2000 B.C., and allegedly traces kingships back 43,200 years.[17] This particular list records kings who lived before and after the flood and who, in some cases, supposedly lived for thousands of years.[18] While this does support the idea that men lived for much longer periods of time before the great Noachic flood, it fails the Bible test by overzealously multiplying the years reported. This was likely because the culture believed that longevity reflected power and they were not afraid to exaggerate truth,[19,20] just as our media and government have no problem with stretching the truth today. The historical importance of the list to modern chronologists is that the kings' names agree with other sources, including the order, even if the dates do not. The Sumerian King List even mentions the flood that covered the earth at one time.[21]

Another list includes the Assyrian Eponym List, which covers more than 300 years from around 900 B.C. to 600 B.C. It specifically names a year in which a total eclipse occurred in Ninevah, which has aided modern astronomers in calculating the precise year (June 15, 763 B.C.) that it occurred according to the Julian calendar system in current use.[22] It also mentions Biblical characters such as King Ahab.[23] This allows a chronologist to match up dates with the Biblical record in order to achieve an extraordinarily high degree of confidence in the dates.

Other Chronologists

Several men have attempted to date and write

about the age of the earth over the years. These include, but are not limited to, Sedar Olam Rabbah, Martin Anstey, Ethelbert Bullinger, Edward Denny, Edwin Thiele, as well as James Ussher and Floyd Nolen Jones mentioned above. All of these men built what they considered a good case for an earth that is between around 5,777 years old and up to around 6,500 years old as of the end of 2016. Naturally, I think I've got the correct calculation nailed down within these pages, but neither did I declare a specific final conclusion. I declared a minimum and maximum range (which is narrower than the range cited above) for the age of the earth, because I do not believe that it is possible to figure out the actual year of creation. I believe the strong case for this inability is simply the fact that God has a master plan that uses a perfect system for time as well as everything else and if we knew the exact date of creation, we might (in theory) be able to figure out the exact date of the end of times from that. God states in His Word that we cannot figure out that final date, so I believe that He does not believe that we need to know the exact beginning date. However, I do believe that we can narrow it down, and know with absolute certainty that the earth (and universe) are not billions, millions, or even 7,000 years old.

Endnotes

1. Jones, Floyd Nolen; *The Chronology of the Old Testament* (Green Forest, AR: Master Books, 2009), xiii.

2. Ussher, James; *The Annals of the World* (Green Forest, AR: Master Books, 2006), 17.

3. Adams, S.C.; *Adams Synchronological Chart* (Green Forest, AR: Master Books, 2007), opening flap.

4. Walton, John; *Chronological and Background*

Charts of the Old Testament (Grand Rapids, MI: Zondervan, 1994), 60.

5. Cooper, Bill; *After the Flood* (West Sussex, England: New Wine Press, 1995).

6. Ibid., 122-123. Cooper says, "...there are certain points on which this early British chronology is patently wrong."

7. Ibid., 124-126. Scaliger used a different dating method, so his conclusion of 4713 B.C. is not likely how we would understand that date, which makes it difficult to know whether he was accurate or not.

8. Ibid., 128. The Mayans used 3113 B.C. as their start date, but their start date corresponded with the great flood, not with creation, so I added 1656 years to their date.

9. Kang, C.H. and Ethel R. Nelson; *The Discovery of Genesis: How the Truths of Genesis were Found Hidden in the Chinese Language* (St. Louis, MO: Concordia Publishing House, 1979), 2. The authors reference Terrien De La Couperie's work, The Language of China Before the Chinese, Taipei, Ch'eng-wen Publishing Co., 1966, page 114, to support this date.

10. *Rose Book of Bible & Christian History Time Lines* (Torrance, CA: Rose Publishing, 2006), first two flaps.

11. Morris, John; "Why Does Nearly Every Culture have a Tradition of a Global Flood?," Institute for Creation Research, 2001,

http://www.icr.org/article/why-does-nearly-every-culture-have-tradition-globa/ (accessed September 15, 2011).

12. Ibid.

13. Ibid.

14. Martin, Charles; (2009), *Flood Legends* (Green

Forest, AR: Master Books, 2009), 10.

15. Cooper, Bill; *After the Flood* (West Sussex, England, New Wine Press, 1995), 146.

16. Ibid., 148.

17. Hoerth, Alfred J.; *Archaeology and the Old Testament* (Grand Rapids, MI: Baker Publishing Group, 2007), 188.

18. Ibid., 189.

19. Merrill, Eugene; (untitled lecture by Dr. Merrill on August 3, 2010), Institute for Creation Research, Dallas, Texas.

20. Merrill, Eugene; *An Historical Survey of the Old Testament* (Grand Rapids, MI: Baker Books, 2009), 60.

21. Hoerth, Alfred J; *Archaeology and the Old Testament* (Grand Rapids, MI: Baker Publishing Group, 2007), 192.

22. Merrill, Eugene; (untitled lecture by Dr. Merrill on August 3, 2010), Institute for Creation Research, Dallas, Texas.

23. Ibid.

CHAPTER 8

FAITH AND LOGIC

Faith is not blind acceptance of silly notions. It is based on reality. It requires proof. Before you start thinking that I am an apostate, please let me explain. The Apostle Paul once wrote:

> *Now faith is the substance of things hoped for, the evidence of things not seen.* Hebrews 11:1

This does not mean that we are to believe in a ghost-like God just because someone tells us we must do so in order to be saved. What it does mean is that we are to interpret the **evidence** that is before us in order to reach the correct conclusion, and much of that evidence is not visible. A few examples might be helpful at this point. Can you see gravity? Absolutely not! However, you can absolutely see its effect. Can you see the wind? No! Nevertheless, you can see its effect. Can you see a seed grow with the naked eye? Can you see a magnetic field? Can you see protons or electrons? No, but you are able to see their effects. Can you see God? No! At least not in the age in which we live today, but we are able to see countless examples of His existence. Consider these Scripture passages:

> *But ask now the beasts, and they shall teach thee; and the fowls of the air, and they shall tell thee: Or speak to the earth, and it shall teach thee: and the fishes of the sea shall declare unto thee. Who knoweth not in all these that the hand of the Lord hath wrought this?* Job 12:7-9

> *For the invisible things of him from the creation of the world are clearly seen, being*

> *understood by the things that are made, even his eternal power and Godhead; so that they are without excuse:* Romans 1:20

So, the Bible testifies that the evidence is right in front of us, but it is by *faith* that we interpret it correctly, just as it is by a different sort of *faith* that the nonbeliever chooses to ignore the evidence or to willfully interpret it wrongly.

Some believe that we must start with human reason in order to reach a conclusion regarding whether God exists or not. This is a half-truth, because if we begin with unfiltered human logic, we end up with a humanistic conclusion that is ungodly. However, if we begin with God-guided reasoning/logic, we are apt to reach excellent conclusions. The trick is that the two types of reasoning are intermixed and difficult to separate, so one must constantly appeal in humility to God for guidance. This is because:

> *The heart is deceitful above all things, and desperately wicked: who can know it?* Jeremiah 17:9

> *For they loved the praise of men more than the praise of God.* John 12:43

So, can logic be trusted? Logic is a set of rules to enable man to think correctly. If, apart from God's Word, one only uses Aristotle's logic, which originates with man, then it will be flawed. Man must first realize that he did not invent logic. He only discovered logic.[1] So, if one understands that God originally set up the rules of logic, then they must be absolute. Those who state that there are no absolutes cannot possibly be correct since the statement that there are no absolutes is an absolute statement. Furthermore, if God is the originator of logic, then He also must be the source and determiner of truth.[2] In fact, since God is truth, then one might say that He is also true logic.[3]

When one examines the thinking behind a man's (or woman's) basis for believing one thing or another, he must necessarily come back at some point to his cumulative 'list' of presuppositions that he has formed in his mind over the course of his life. Some claim that they believe that Jesus Christ is their Savior and yet they also say that the earth is billions of years old. This indirectly violates the logical Law of Non-contradiction, so one statement must be false. The Law of Non-contradiction states that two contradictory statements cannot both be true. The above two statements are contradictory because Christ taught (in an answer to a question from a group of Pharisees):

> *And he answered and said unto them, Have ye not read, that he which made them at the beginning made them male and female.* Matthew 19:4

As I made clear in Chapter One, the beginning was the start of all creation. In Chapter Two, I covered the inerrancy of Scripture and why it must be true and in Chapter Six, the time line through the ages. So, if one believes in Christ, but does not believe His Word, then there is a disconnect in the logic. Likewise, if one believes in the inerrancy of the Bible, but does not believe in Christ, it simply does not make sense. True (God-granted) logic *must* make sense.

The 'logic of faith' leads us to understand that the original Scripture is inerrant and infallible.[4] Edward F. Hills put it this way:

> If God has not preserved the Scriptures by His special providence, why would He have infallibly inspired them in the first place? And if it is not important that the Scriptures be regarded as infallibly inspired, why is it

> important to insist that the Gospel is completely true? And if this is not important, why is it important to believe that Jesus is the divine Son of God? In short, unless we follow the logic of faith, we can be certain of nothing concerning the Bible and its text.[5]

Continuing this line of thinking, it becomes clear that it is actually not even possible to possess real knowledge of anything without having a reason for it.[6] That is because a belief must be totally true in order for it to be considered general knowledge[7] and because "knowledge is true, *justified* belief."[8] So, a non-Christian who believes that the earth is billions of years old accounts for this by flawed reasoning. He does so within his own unbiblical worldview, yet he cannot account for his own ability to reason.[9] However, a young-earth creationist can reason and account for his ability to reason from a Biblical worldview, because he can explain where his reasoning ability originated. Furthermore, since a young-earth creationist is consistent and not arbitrary in his reasoning, then his knowledge is based on truth (because there are only two principal views of the age of the earth—billions of years versus thousands of years).

Logical Fallacies

There are several means by which people delude themselves or fool others by way of bad logic. Moreover, there are some good books written on this topic, so I only intend to briefly discuss a few of the most common logical fallacies that I have observed being used by writers and speakers regarding the present topic. First, it is quite common for a scientist or academic to write or say something like, "This must be true because most experts agree..." A red flag should go up in the reader's mind every time he sees or hears such a statement. This is a classical fallacy known as an "appeal to the majority."[10] It is sometimes called *conclusion by consensus* or *consensus science*. Either way, it is not logical. Some might try to argue that the majority of scientists could not be wrong, but, in point of fact, the majority of scientists and other groups have been wrong on numerous occasions. One well-known example is the belief by most experts in the 1500s that the sun revolved around the earth. Galileo Galilei confronted the majority on this point and was ostracized by the Roman Catholic church and given a life sentence of house arrest.[11] The late Michael Critchton, who was no friend of creationism, addressed the issue of consensus science best in a lecture at the California Institute for Technology in 2003,

> "...I want to pause here and talk about this notion of consensus, and the rise of what has been called consensus science. I regard consensus science as an extremely pernicious development that ought to be stopped cold in its tracks. Historically, the claim of consensus has been the first refuge of scoundrels; it is a way to avoid debate by claiming that the matter is already settled. Whenever you hear the consensus of scientists agrees on something or other, reach for your wallet, because you're being had.
>
> Let's be clear: The work of science has nothing whatever to do with consensus. Consensus is the business of politics. Science, on the contrary, requires only one investigator who happens to be right, which means that he or she has results that are verifiable by reference to the real world. In science, consensus is irrelevant. What is relevant is reproducible results. The greatest scientists in

> history are great precisely because they broke with the consensus. There is no such thing as consensus science. If it's consensus, it isn't science. If it's science, it isn't consensus. Period. . . .
>
> I would remind you to notice where the claim of consensus is invoked. Consensus is invoked only in situations where the science is not solid enough. Nobody says the consensus of scientists agrees that $E=mc^2$. Nobody says the consensus is that the sun is 93 million miles away. It would never occur to anyone to speak that way..."[12]

A second common fallacy is known as the "appeal to authority"[13] which is similar to the previous fallacy, since the appeal to the majority usually involves some reference to the idea that the majority thinks as it does because the experts say they should believe as such. By the authority fallacy, writers and speakers appeal to the expertise of those with advanced degrees and/or many years of experience in a field. However, it really does not matter one iota how much experience or how many advanced degrees a person holds when it comes to being assured of the soundness of an argument. Neither does it matter how good a scholar's vocabulary happens to be. In the final analysis, all that really matters is whether the argument is true, and we know from previous chapters, that the sole source of truth originates with God. Nevertheless, I have often seen people overcome with the 'eloquence of the expert' phenomena. This usually manifests itself by way of an individual who might hold a Ph.D., or who speaks or writes in such a way as to impress and/or intimidate. As a result, the reader may be so impressed that he accepts the 'expert's' statement as truth without questioning and without being furnished with real evidence.

A third common logical fallacy is that of the 'prejudices.'[14] Isaac Watts explained one type of prejudice as *credo quia impossible est* or "I believe it, because it is impossible."[15] Which really means, 'I believe something else, because this argument is impossible.' In other words, many academics refuse to believe that God is tripartite because they see it as impossible. What they really mean, although they usually will not admit it, is that they do not understand how God can be triune, and they require a human explanation (humanism) to convince them of any argument. This is in spite of the myriad of 'threes' in our universe, which serve as imperfect analogies, but may help with our understanding, such as the triple point of water (H_2O can coexist as a solid, liquid and gas, depending on whether the temperature and pressure are just right), or that music has melody, harmony, and rhythm, or that an atom has three principle parts—neutrons, protons, and electrons (all must be in place to make mass (take up space)). There are many more examples.

A fourth fallacy that is regularly repeated is known as the *ad hominem* attack.[16] This is one of the most commonly used methods that I have observed on on-line computer threads, web logs, and comments or postings on websites. In this false way of thinking, the writer attacks the person instead of the argument. I have also observed it used regularly in the political arena. Unfortunately, many an unwary person has taken the bait and agreed to chase a rabbit trail away from the central argument and the two (or more) debaters soon find themselves far away from the original issue, which is exactly where the initiator of the *ad hominem* false logic desired to end up. I have also observed on many occasions that the person under attack resorted to the same tactics, and the argument was quickly spun off the central issue. My personal thought on this is to avoid arguing with such persons. Consider what the Bible says about this:

> *Give not that which is holy unto the dogs, neither cast ye your pearls before swine, lest they trample them under their feet, and turn again and rend you.* Matthew 7:6
>
> *Answer not a fool according to his folly, lest thou also be like unto him.* Proverbs 26:4

In other words, if a young-earth creationist involves himself in an argument in which he is attacked on an *ad hominem* basis, he will be wasting his time, because the attacker is blind and will only escalate the passion of the argument for no practical purpose other than to irritate. This is not to say that we should never attempt to involve ourselves in discussions which may result in a dead end, but that we should pull away once it is recognized for what it is because it is like chasing the wind to argue with a person who is illogical.

The next common method of incorrect thinking that I will address is that of the "straw man fallacy."[17] This is so common that I have seen it used by ignorant news media types on a regular basis. In this fallacy, a person misrepresents the position of his opponent. He sets up an invisible straw man of sorts to argue with and against, in lieu of his opponent's true position. The argument itself might be very persuasive, but if it is not directed to the principal issue, then it must be deemed a straw man fallacy. One of the reasons that the straw man fallacy is so common among the unknowing is that they really do not understand and are not very familiar with what their opponents think or teach. For example, it seems to me that most media types who attack young-earth creationism have never carefully examined the assumptions behind old earth (billions of years) thinking, nor are they familiar with the overwhelming volume of evidence supporting an earth that is just a few thousand years old. Instead, they rely on arguments from friends and/or so-called experts (appeal to authority) to defend their wayward thinking. And, sometimes being pressed to meet a deadline, they are simply too lazy to do their homework properly.

The last fallacy that I will address in this chapter is that of "begging the question."[18] This fallacy in thinking is based on an argument which presupposes the conclusion. It is also known as circular reasoning. For example, one might say, "I know he is a boy because his name is Homer." Admittedly, it might seem highly likely that Homer is a boy, because the name is commonly given to males, and you may not know of a single instance of any female in the world by that name. However, I once knew a woman named Homer (personally), and so I can attest that sometimes women are named Homer. Does this change the thinking? It might change the viewpoint of the reader, but it does not change the fact that it is fallaciously illogical to argue a point circularly. The only entity in the known universe who is allowed to argue tautologically is God Himself. "How could this be?" you might ask. Why should God be allowed an exception?

First, God created all things including logic, so that means He sets the rules. Second, God cannot lie.

> *In hope of eternal life, which God, that cannot lie, promised before the world began;*
> Titus 1:2

Third, God is neither arbitrary nor capricious. He is consistent and rational. Even if we do not understand what He did or is doing, He knows what He is doing. Fourth, God really does not ever argue tautologically, but sometimes we think He does because, either we do not understand His thinking (because our minds are finite), or He chooses not to reveal certain things to us. This is supported as follows:

> *For my thoughts are not your thoughts, neither are your ways my ways, saith the Lord. For as the heavens are higher than the earth, so are my ways higher than your ways, and my thoughts than your thoughts.* Isaiah 55:8-9

> *The secret things belong unto the Lord our God.* Deuteronomy 29:29

So, in the final analysis, God alone reasons however He chooses. However, He is always rational and true even if we have difficulty following His logic at times. On the other hand, man, being sinful even when he is at his best, must necessarily be occasionally arbitrary, irrational, or wrong. Only the books of the Bible are inerrant (because they are inspired by God). Other writings by the Biblical authors almost certainly were not inerrant and that would be one reason why God chose not to preserve them.

There are many other logical fallacies and the reader who is serious about understanding correct thinking should spend some time becoming familiar with many of these. The few fallacies described above are those that I find to be the most common among those who prefer to believe that the thinking of men trumps that of God's perfect logic.

Endnotes

1. Chittick, Donald E.; *The Puzzle of Ancient Man* (Newberg, OR: Creation Compass, 2006), 220.

2. Clark, Gordon; *Logic* (Unicoi, TN: The Trinity Foundation, 2004), 114.

3. Ibid., 115-117.

4. Jones, Floyd Nolen; *Which Version is the Bible?* (Goodyear, AZ: Kingsword Press, 2006), 211. Jones cites Edward F. Hill's book, *The King James Version Defended*, page 192.

5. Ibid., 211. Jones cites Edward F. Hill's book, *The King James Version Defended*, page 225.

6. Lisle, Jason; *The Ultimate Proof of Creation* (Green Forest, AR: Master Books, 2009), 41.

7. Ibid.

8. Ibid.

9. Ibid., 53.

10. Ibid., 122.

11. Hannam, James; *The Genesis of Science* (Washington, DC: Regnery Publishing, Inc., 2011), 323, 333-334.

12. Critchton, Michael; "Aliens Cause Global Warming," 2003, Wall Street Journal, http://online.wsj.com/article/SB122603134258207975.html (accessed August 30, 2011).

13. McDurmon Joel; *Biblical Logic in Theory and Practice* (Powder Springs, GA: The American Vision, Inc., 2009), 245.

14. Watts, Isaac; *Logic* (Grand Rapids, MI: Soli Deo Gloria Publications, 2008), 179.

15. Ibid., 205.

16. McDurmon, Joel; *Biblical Logic in Theory and Practice* (Powder Springs, GA: The American Vision, Inc., 2009), 315.

17. Lisle, Jason, *The Ultimate Proof of Creation* (Green Forest, AR: Master Books, 2009), 125.

18. Ibid., 113.

CHAPTER 9

A FEW STATISTICAL EVIDENCES

In this chapter, I have listed a number of statistical proofs supporting the fact that the earth is not more than 6,300 years old. While some might consider these proofs to be circumstantial, they fully corroborate evidence from the inerrant Bible that the earth is not older than said years. While it is not my intent to present an exhaustive list of statistical evidences of a young earth, the cumulative effect of the forensic evidence elucidates the truth of the earth's real age.

Population Growth

What should the population on earth be if the Biblical view were true (and it is)? Since the Biblical view includes having nearly all the population being destroyed by a global deluge during Noah's day, it follows that a population calculation should start from that point, since no catastrophe of that magnitude has been recorded since that time. Remembering that the time of the Noachic deluge was around 1,656 years after creation, we can subtract that from the number 6,025 (the estimated age of the earth) and arrive at an approximate Noachic flood date of about 4,369 years ago.

The key factor in this calculation is deciding what number should be assumed for population growth. If the population grew at 2% a year, starting with just two persons (Noah and his wife), then it would only take about 1,100 years to reach 6,000,000,000 people[1] (the approximate population on earth today is around 7,500,000,000). While the growth rate of populations in some countries does exceed 2% per year at times, there are times when negative growth occurs due to war, famine, and disease. Other reasons for negative population growth include parents choosing not to have children (or having fewer children), abortion,[2] homosexuality, infanticide, euthanasia, and government restrictions for population control purposes.[3] What if we calculate the growth of the population at an average rate of 1% a year? After only 3,300 years the population would have equaled the present population on earth.[4] What if we assume an average growth rate of 0.5% per year? This calculation easily yields a population that is approximately what it is today[5], and yet, it is only about one-fourth of the current population growth rate on earth. This exercise demonstrates that not only is it possible to end up with a large population from only two people in 4,369 years (or less) even though there were in actuality eight persons living and procreating after the flood ended; it also shows that the population is likely to be what it is today when death, due to various causes, stymies population growth from time to time, through the ages.

The Earth's Magnetic Field

Scientists began measuring the earth's magnetic field in 1829. Over a period of years, it has been discovered that this magnetic field is losing its intensity on an exponential basis. Further studies of 'archaeomagnetism' (the study of the magnetism in pottery, bricks and the like, from the past) reveal that around 1,000 years ago the earth's magnetic field was approximately 40% stronger than it is today. Additionally, it has been decaying steadily since then.[6]

The challenge is to extrapolate the magnetic field back in time to some point when the intensity would have been too great for life to have been sustainable. If the magnetic 'curve' was extrapolated back 7,000 years, the magnetic field intensity would have been 32 times greater than it is today[7]; it really could not have been much stronger than that since the earth would have melted from the heat of the core.[8] However, it is also known that the magnetic field fluctuated quite a bit about the time of the Noachic flood.[9] These fluctuations are combined, with the extrapolated curve on a graph, thanks to Dr. Russell Humphreys, to illustrate how this might have looked (see graph A).[10]

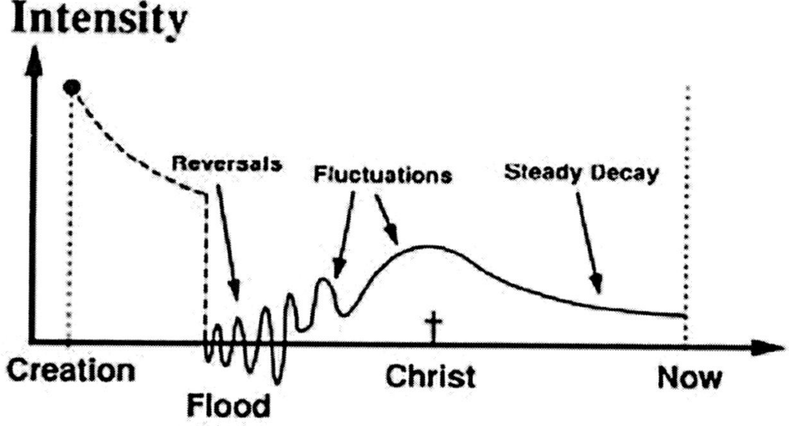

Figure 1. Magnetic field intensity at the earth's surface, from creation to now.

Graph A

In the final analysis, considering the fluctuations, the steady decay and the time having passed, the loss of intensity in earth's magnetic field agrees strongly with an earth that was created about 6,000 years ago.[11] Furthermore, the near-term consequences of the diminishing magnetic field appear to validate a bleak outlook for earth's future.

Comet Life

Still another evidence that the earth cannot be older than a few thousand years is that of comet decay. Many comets have died out over the years and others are near death because they are all in the process of breaking up.[12] Comets are simply made up of rocks and dust surrounded by ice.[13] They must disintegrate over time since they are always moving, which creates heat energy, which in turn slowly melts off the comet. In general, comets cannot last more than a few thousand years because of this melt off.[14] Some scientists have tried to invent an alternative explanation for comets so that they can 'prove' that the universe is billions of years old through such notions as the totally conjectural Oort cloud (an alleged source of new comets).[15] However, while the Oort cloud idea now shows up in textbooks, there is not one tiny bit of evidence to support its existence. It is a mere invention of one man's imagination—Jan Oort.[16, 17] This is one area that I did not address in the chapter on logic; made up 'facts.' It would seem that people could see through false facts, but unfortunately that is often not the case. Perhaps this is more easily understood when one considers Adolf Hitler's words from his book, *Mein Kampf*:

> "The size of the lie is a definite factor in causing it to be believed, for the vast masses of a nation are in the depths of their hearts more easily deceived than they are consciously and intentionally bad. The primitive simplicity of their minds renders them a more easy prey to a big lie than a small one, for they themselves often tell little lies, but would be ashamed to tell big lies."[18]

How did Hitler fool so many millions of people in the 1930s? How is it that our own government is able to deceive millions into believing that we do not need to cut expenditures, but must continually raise the 'debt ceiling?' Perhaps it's the same reason people find it so easy to believe that the earth is billions of years old.

Mutations

The human genome is the biological entity which encompasses the entirety of a person's genetic code. It is made of over three billion DNA (deoxyribonucleic acid) base pairs. It is extremely complex and no scientist has any valid idea how it could have evolved from a single cell organism (because it didn't). The fact is, man is formed in such a way that his genetic information must decay over time.[19] When a piece of genetic information is passed to the next generation, it sometimes mutates (an error is originated in the hereditary gene(s)). This probably began after the fall of Adam and Eve in the garden of Eden.

If we start with a diploid genome size of six billion, it can be expected that about one ten millionth of our hereditary information is lost each generation. What is incredible about this is that a single computer error can shut down an entire electronic machine or even a network system. Yet, the human genetic code is so robust that it can handle quite a few 'errors' (mutations). Conversely, if there were too many mutations, the human race would cease to exist.[20]

The actual rate of all types of mutations has been estimated at more than 600 per person per generation. At this rate, for 300 generations (6,000 years), we would expect to acquire about 90,000 errors (0.003%) per human body, and yet, we continue to be viable as a human race. On the other hand, if the cumulative mutation rate were much higher, we humans would no longer be functional.[21] Perhaps this is a message as much about the looming end times as it is about the youth of the earth itself. Considering this fact in conjunction with the study regarding the decay of earth's magnetic field, there is reason for pause to cogitate on one's status with regard to the future.

The Sun

According to a scholarly paper by Keith Davies, the sun possesses characteristics of a heavenly body that is a mere several thousand years old.[22] First, it holds evidence by way of the element lithium. Extremely hot lithium should all be burned up and gone in 7,500 years; yet, the sun apparently still has about 1,000th of its original abundance of this element.[23] The sun also has an abundance of the element beryllium which should not be there at all if the sun were 15 billion years old, as some suppose.[24] There are a couple of other more technical reasons that the age of the sun is consistent with an approximately 6,000-year-old universe, including its neutrino emission and its oscillation.[25]

Other evidence that the sun is young includes a study completed in 1980 which indicates that the sun is shrinking (being burned up) at the rate of about 0.1% per century.[26] The diameter of the sun is about 1,000,000 miles (compared to the entire circumference of the earth which is a mere 24,902 miles). So, 6,000 years ago, the sun would have been about 6% larger than it is today, which would still have supported life on earth. However, if the sun were much older and larger, it would not support life due to the fact that it would be too hot on earth[27] for humans to survive.

Endnotes

1. Morris, Henry M. and John D. Morris; *The Modern Creation Trilogy, Volume II* (Green Forest, AR: Master Books, 1996), 317.

2. Grant, George; *Killer Angel* (Nashville, TN: Cumberland House Publishing, 2001), 19. Grant states that Margaret Sanger, the founder of Planned Parenthood, was responsible through her organization

for the murder by abortion of over 30 million babies in the United States and 2,500,000,000 worldwide (all in the last 90 years up to 2001).

3. Ibid., 318.

4. Ferrell, Vance; *The Evolution Handbook* (Altamont, TN: Evolution Facts, Inc, 2005), 156.

5. Snelling, Andrew A.; *Earth's Catastrophic Past, vol. 1* (Dallas, TX: Institute for Creation Research, 2009), 67.

6. Humphreys, Russell D.; "The Earth's Magnetic Field is Young," Institute for Creation Research, 1993, http://www.icr.org/article/earths-magnetic-field-young/ (accessed August 15, 2011).

7. Morris, Henry M. and John D. Morris; *The Modern Creation Trilogy, Volume II* (Green Forest, AR: Master Books, 1996), 323.

8. Snelling, Andrew A.; *Earth's Catastrophic Past, vol. 2* (Dallas, TX: Institute for Creation Research, 2009), 873.

9. Humphreys, Russell D.; "The Earth's Magnetic Field is Young," Institute for Creation Research, 1993, http://www.icr.org/article/earths-magnetic-field-young/ (accessed August 15, 2011).

10. Ibid.

11.Snelling, Andrew A.; *Earth's Catastrophic Past, vol. 2* (Dallas, TX: Institute for Creation Research, 2009), 873.

12. Morris, Henry M. and John D. Morris; *The Modern Creation Trilogy, Volume II* (Green Forest, AR: Master Books, 1996), 326-327.

13. Lawrence, Debbie and Richard Lawrence; *God's Design for Heaven and Earth: Our Universe* (Windsor, CO: R and D Publishing Center, LLC, 2003), 36.

14. Ibid., 37.

15. Humphreys, Russell "Evidence for a Young World," Institute for Creation Research, 2005, http://www.icr.org/article/evidence-for-young-world/ (accessed September 1, 2011).

16. Snelling, Andrew A.; *Earth's Catastrophic Past, vol. 2* (Dallas, TX: Institute for Creation Research, 2009), 871.

17. Morris, John; *The Young Earth* (Green Forest, AR: Master Books, 2007), 20.

18. Hitler, Adolf; Infamous Adolf Hitler Quote, Liberty-Tree (translated from German), 2008, http://quotes.liberty-tree.ca/quote_blog/Adolf.Hitler. Quote.3417.

19. Sanford, J.C.; *Genetic Entropy and the Mystery of the Genome* (Waterloo, NY: FMS Publications, 2008), 152.

20. Ibid., 153.

21. Ibid.

22. Davies, Keith; "Evidence for a Young Sun," Institute for Creation Research, 1996, http://www.icr.org/article/evidence-for-young-sun/ (accessed September 5, 2011).

23. Ibid.

24. Ibid.

25. Ibid.

26. Akridge, Russell; "The Sun is Shrinking," Institute for Creation Research, 1980, http://www.icr.org/article/sun-shrinking/ (accessed September 5, 2011).

27. Ibid. If there were some sort of protective barrier in or above the atmosphere to dissipate the heat, it would have made life more tolerable during the antediluvian period and there is a distinct possibility that this was the case.

CHAPTER 10

A FEW EMPIRICAL EVIDENCES

In 1997, an eight-year research program was initiated by a group of scientists who saw some of the problems inherent in the dating methodologies and in the assumed age of the earth.[1] This study covered a number of important topics, but we will examine only a few here.

First of all, it was concluded from several studies that a large amount of radioactive decay has occurred at a time or times in the past. This was primarily based on observations of fission tracks made on a number of rock samples taken from around the United States and on studies of radiohalos (discolored spheres of radioactive damage) in granites from all over the world.[2]

In one of the most significant research projects of this program, the Radioisotopes and the Age of the Earth (RATE) team examined the diffusion of helium in zirconium silicate (also known as zircon). Helium is a slippery gas and should not remain in the zircons after millions or billions of years. Nevertheless, it does exist, and it is reasonable and expected for it to remain in the zircons after only a few thousand years. In this project, Dr. Russell Humphreys suggested that the rate of decay of ^{238}U was accelerated at some time or times in the recent past which would have caused a considerable number of alpha-particles (helium) to have been emitted from the radioactive nuclides. The remaining amount of helium harmonized well with Dr. Humphreys' calculations, which projected an estimated 6,000-year-old earth.[3]

In another research project, Dr. Andrew Snelling

examined a large quantity of radiohalos in minerals from around the world. He found a considerable number of polonium radiohalos isolated from their parent isotopes. He posited that the polonium isotopes or their immediate parents, the radon isotopes (which do not emit alpha particles) and which exhibit very short half-lives, had been transported by hydrothermal fluids during a time when the temperature was rapidly cooling from above 150 degrees Centigrade. When the temperature cooled sufficiently to "freeze" the clusters of polonium nuclides around sulfur, for which it has an affinity, they left "stamps" of evidence for future researchers to study. Nearby were many ^{238}U radiohalos that were fully formed and matured without the expected polonium concentric rings within the said spheres of radiohalos of uranium. Snelling concluded that the decay rate of uranium must have been accelerated in order to accommodate this phenomenon since all isotopes of polonium experience fairly short half-lives and could not have been transported in the same rocks within millimeters of fully-formed uranium radiohalos without a rapidly-cooling, catastrophic event accompanied by accelerated nuclear decay of the parent(s).[4]

In the last RATE project cited in this work, Dr. John Baumgardner completed an examination of the amount of ^{14}C in diamonds—one of the densest and hardest minerals known to man. ^{14}C has a half-life of 5,730 years and there should not be a measurable trace of it in anything claimed to be really old (millions of years) after about ten half-lives, but fair quantities of ^{14}C were found in diamonds which were previously believed to be very old (millions of years). Dr. Baumgardner ruled out contamination as a reason for the ^{14}C being detected in such amounts since the readings were in excess of the threshold for the laboratory equipment, and the measuring techniques are substantially more accurate today than they were just 50 years ago. Also, since diamonds are so dense, the probability of contamination over the years is nil.[5]

These studies and others are evidence of the scientific method in action—observation, development of a hypothesis, testability and interpretation of results.[6] Of course, when interpreting the past, there can never be an absolute observation or test. However, by studying geochronology, conducting experiments designed to minimize assumptions, and interpreting the data with a Biblical worldview, scientists are more likely to reach conclusions that are not in conflict with the observed data.

Red Blood Cells and Soft Tissue in Fossil Remains

In 2005, Mary Schweitzer, a paleontologist, discovered the fossil remains of a Tyrannosaurus rex in Montana. After returning to her laboratory in North Carolina, she dissolved some of the fragments in an acid and looked at the resultant specimens under a microscope. What she observed was living red blood cells and soft tissue.[7] Red blood cells and soft tissue cannot exist for more than a few thousand years,[8] so this has caused quite a large problem for those who support evolutionary ideas (claiming that man and dinosaurs did not coexist and that the last dinosaur became extinct about 65 million years ago). Then a few years later, a Hadrosaur fossil was discovered in Montana. It too had blood cells intact that had survived decomposition.[9] The fact that biological materials simply decay way too fast to support anything older than a few thousand years is well established.[10]

Then again, in a third example, not very long ago, a piece of lizard skin and the connecting tissue was found in the Green River Formation which covers parts of Wyoming and northern Colorado.[11] This is a fossil bed that is alleged to be 40 million years old. How could this be? Clearly, someone is wrong. When evaluated in conjunction with other empirical evidence, and by dovetailing it with the Biblical version of history, one can reach no other reasonable conclusion except that these creatures were buried and died during or after the Noachic Flood which was about 4,300 years ago (see Chapter 6).

Tree Rings

Dendrochronology is the study of dating by tree rings. It is an interesting and complex discipline. One of the modern discoveries of the dendrochronologists is that the oldest living trees on earth are the Bristlecone pines which make their home in the White Mountains of eastern California.[12] Of the various Bristlecone pines, there is one which has been appropriately named Methuselah, because it is purported to be the oldest living example of flora on the planet at an alleged 4,600 years.[13] It was reported to have had 4,789 rings in the late 1950s.[14] Of course, if one assumes one ring of growth per year, then this would date it earlier than the great flood of Noah's day which likely killed all vegetation excepting seed material. However, remembering that we should filter all information through the Bible first and then seek the answers that agree with the Biblical view, and upon further review, it is found that the number of tree rings is not a problem at all for a flood that was only about 4,300 years ago. In point of fact, it has been demonstrated that sometimes trees grow several rings in a single year.[15] The reality is that tree rings can be a witness to wet and dry seasons (or periods of time) and are not proof of months or calendar years having passed.

Additionally, other factors can alter the rings as

John Woodmorappe explains in an article from *Answers in Genesis,*

> "It has long been known that individual tree rings can be changed, during growth, from the climate-signal-dictated size to a different size as a result of some disturbance. This disturbance (for example, insect attack, earthquake, release of gas, etc.) can make the ring either smaller or larger. If these disturbances occurred at sufficient frequency, and reappeared in sequence in other trees at later times, the actually-contemporaneous trees would cross-match in an age-staggered manner, thus creating an artificial chronology."[16]

In a second example, the Redwood Sequoias of California are possibly the second oldest trees on earth.[17] The oldest ones have been dated at between 3,000 and 4,000 years.[18] Counting rings in a Sequoia is somewhat easier than counting them in a Bristlecone pine because they are so much larger in diameter; hence, some experts believe it is the most accurate dating by dendrochronology that exists.[19]

Entropy

One of the basic laws of the universe is that the total quantity of matter is constant. Mass can change to energy or vice-versa, but it cannot go away or increase on its own. This means that nothing new is created by present processes. Another universal law known as the Second Law of Thermodynamics states that there is a tendency for all things to disintegrate or move toward disorder.

Let's suppose you clean up your room or your office and you leave it in absolutely perfect order for 100 years and then return. What can you expect? First, you can expect a layer of dust all over the room and its contents. Second, anything that was exposed to oxygen, sunlight and moisture will have decayed a bit if not a lot. Paper becomes brittle and the air becomes stale smelling. Let's say you abandoned your room for four millennia. Would you expect it to remain in perfect order? If it were air-right, and little to no moisture was allowed into the room, you might actually expect your papers to survive. If not, it is very unlikely that they would have been preserved. Now, suppose you allowed a four-year-old in your room for 15 minutes. What would happen? Perhaps 4,000 years worth of disorder could be accomplished in a quarter hour!

The concept is the same with our universe. There is no such thing as order increasing within the universe except through intelligent intervention, and that is a temporary action in itself, because whatever is put in order will once again prefer to move toward disorder. The point is that the universe has a limited life. It had a beginning about 6,000 years ago and it will have an end. Based on some of the studies outlined in this chapter, I think it is reasonable to assume that our universe is approaching the end of its life cycle unless there is Divine intervention. When it will end I cannot know, but I know how it will end. The book of 2 Peter helps us here:

> *But the day of the Lord will come as a thief in the night; in the which the heavens shall pass away with a great noise, and the elements shall melt with fervent heat, the earth also and the works that are therein shall be burned up. 2 Peter 3:10*

So, global warming is true after all. The end of the world as we know it will involve a lot of heat and it won't be fun for those who perish for failing to trust Christ as Savior. For believers, perhaps now would be a good time to consider the question: What have I done for the cause of Christ—lately?

Endnotes

1. Vardiman, Larry, Andrew A. Snelling, and Eugene E. Chaffin, ed.; *Radioisotopes and the Age of the Earth, Volume II: The Results of a Young-Earth Creationist Initiative* (El Cajon, CA and Chino Valley AZ: Institute for Creation Research and Creation Research Society, 2005), 1-2.

2. Ibid., 209-210.

3. Ibid., 56,74-75.

4. Ibid., 146-149.

5. Ibid., 623-624.

6. Morris, John; *The Young Earth* (Green Forest, AR: Master Books, 2007), 14-15.

7. Helen Fields, "Dinosaur Shocker," Smithsonian, 2006, http://www.printthis.clickability.com/pt/cpt?expire=&title=Dinosaur+Shocker+%7C+Science+%26+Nature+%7C+Smithsonian+Magazine&urlID=24615171&action=cpt&partnerID=253167&cid=10021606&fb=Y&url=http%3A%2F%2Fwww.smithsonianmag.com%2Fscience-nature%2Fdinosaur.html (accessed September 2, 2011).

8. Thomas, Brian; "Hadrosaur Soft Tissues Another Blow to Long-Ages Myth," Institute for Creation Research, 2009, http://www.icr.org/article/hadrosaur-soft-tissues-another-blow/ (accessed September 2, 2011).

9. Ibid.

10. Humphreys, Russell; "Evidence for a Young World," Institute for Creation Research, 2005, http://www.icr.org/article/evidence-for-young-world/ (accessed September 1, 2011).

11. Thomas, Brian; "Green River Formation has Original Soft Tissue," Institute for Creation Research, 2011,http://www.icr.org/article/green-river-formation-fossil-has-original/ (accessed September 2, 2011).

12. Lorey, Frank; "Tree Rings and Biblical Chronology," Institute for Creation Research, 1994, http://www.icr.org/article/tree-rings-biblical-chronology/ (accessed September 9, 2011).

13. Ibid.

14. Thomas, Brian; "Why Aren't Earth's Oldest Trees Older?," Institute for Creation Research, 2010, http://www.icr.org/article/why-arent-earths-oldest-trees-older/ (accessed September 9, 2011).

15. Ibid.

16. Woodmorappe, John; "Biblical Chronology and the 8,000-Year-Long Bristlecone Pine Tree-Ring Chronology," Answers in Genesis, 2009, http://www.answersingenesis.org/articles/aid/v4/n1/biblical-chronology-bristlecone-pine (accessed September 9, 2011).

17. Robbins, Dorothy E. Kreiss; "Can the Redwoods Date the Flood?," Institute for Creation Research, 1984, http://www.icr.org/article/can-redwoods-date-flood/ (accessed September 9, 2011).

18. Ibid.

19. Ibid.

CHAPTER 11

PALEONTOLOGICAL EVIDENCE

Over the last few hundred years, several thousand ancient human skeletons have been located and identified[1] from all around the world. Does this find correlate with an earth that is a few thousand years old? Most long-age anthropologists believe that man lived for at least 185,000 years before farming began. If they habitually buried their dead, it has been calculated that they would have buried approximately eight billion bodies.[2] Clearly this does not make sense in light of the few remains that have been found. The difference between eight billion and a few thousand is enormous. However, the numbers do agree with an earth that is about 6,000 years old, with a global deluge having occurred about 4,300 years ago that drowned nearly all humans living at that time. Unburied bodies are known to bloat and float, which would explain why not many skeletal remains are found today since most, if not all, of these bodies would have experienced rapid decay, leaving very little evidence of their existence for modern scientists to find. Moreover, it is just plain silly to think that man would not figure out how to farm for 185,000 years. After all, many of the human bones that have been found buried also have man-made artifacts buried with them.[3] This is an indication of intelligence, which makes it laughable for evolutionary paleontologists to assume that man didn't discover agricultural ideas for 185,000 years. The Biblical model fits neatly, whereby God taught Adam and Eve to farm and they passed their knowledge on to their progeny. Noah and his sons would have had this knowledge when they entered the ark, and they would have passed on their skill sets to their own children and grandchildren.

What about non-human fossils? Contrary to popular belief, large amounts of time are not required to form fossils.[4] All fossil-forming processes happen relatively quickly (within days, months, and years; not millions of years). An example of permineralization was illustrated by suspending teddy bears under dripping lime-rich water in England. The bears took approximately three months to fossilize.[5] An example of petrification occurs often with wooden support poles which are regularly replaced in the canals of Venice, Italy.[6]

Ninety-five percent of all fossils are marine invertebrates, and most are shellfish. Of the remaining five percent, 95% are algae and plant fossils (4.75%). Ninety-five percent of the remaining 0.25% consists of the other invertebrates, including insects (0.2375%). The remaining 0.0125% includes all vertebrates, which are mostly fish. Very few land vertebrates have ever been found and most of them consist of less than one bone. Ninety-five percent of the mammal fossils were deposited during the Ice Age (following the global Noachic flood). Essentially all the marine fossils are found on the continents (almost none in the oceans).[7] How do we explain this? By means of a great cataclysmic watery event that utterly annihilated the continents and land dwellers (see Genesis 7:18-24; 2 Peter 3:6). Why else would marine fossils be found ALL over the globe and on top of mountains?

The Geologic Column

Fossil remains are usually found in what is known as the geologic column. The geologic column is a secular paleosystem that was developed to identify the age of fossils by their commonality within a given layer of solidified sediment and to identify the geologic layers (and ages of the layers) by the fossils held within said layers.[8] This is tautological and fails as a method for this reason alone, because the secular evolutionists have pre-decided the ages of the layers/fossils without any good evidence based on the scientific method. The whole system reeks of a pyramid of presuppositional assumptions that lacks a viable foundation.

On the other hand, creationists have taken this secular system and modified it to use it to identify zones of pre-flood, mid-flood, and post-flood sediment movement.[9] As an example, creationists would say that the dinosaur zone is within the Mesozoic "Era" which includes the Cretaceous, Jurassic and Triassic layers. This is congruent with the apparent reality that the great majority of fossilized remains of dinosaurs are found within these sedimentary layers. The evolutionists would say that the dinosaur age is found within the Mesozoic Era, but their conclusion, which is untenable, states that because most dinosaur fossils are found within these layers then the age of the layer is between 65 million years of age and 245 million years of age.

Creationists use the column to identify commonality of fossils and to approximate when a layer was laid down by water/mud (early, mid, late, or even post-flood), and evolutionists use it to date the age of the earth in millions of years and to define approximately "when" creatures evolved. Creationists also use the column to identify what ecologies might have lived together in the past (which are very similar to what we have today, excepting extinct creatures and plants).

The sequencing of the layers in the column is 'useful' to evolutionists for dating the layers or the fossils for whatever purpose they need or want.

Creationists use the sequencing to try to unravel the mystery of the flood environment in hopes of finding how life might have been in the pre-flood era (i.e., extra-large animals such as dinosaurs, giant beavers, etc., moderate year-round temperatures, higher amounts of CO_2 and higher atmospheric pressure). It is also useful as a powerful witness regarding the veracity of Scripture (evidence of a global deluge).

Evolutionists *assume* that the first appearances of fossils (called FAD by scientists) could be due to their first occurrence as an "evolved" animal and they *assume* that last appearances of fossils in the strata (called LAD by scientists) are the last occurrences of an animal just before it became extinct. While some animals have clearly become extinct, most have not, and we mostly see the same animals today as existed before the flood (perhaps with more genetic defects, but still the same kinds of animals).

To further clarify this, creationists understand that first (lowest) appearances of fossils are those that were buried in the flood first by underwater mudslides (at the lowest elevations), and then by other types of mudslides, pyroclastic flows and settlements of debris, dust and dirt during and after the flood. Of course, the low-laying marine dwellers got buried first because they were already at the bottom of the oceans (lowest elevations). Other creatures and plant life were buried in sequence according to their ecology, topography (elevation), and mobility. The last in sequence to be buried would have been the most mobile (having ability to flee to higher ground and possibly the most intelligent) and/or lived on higher ground (unless a mudslide caused them to slide down to a lower level and become buried).

According to evolutionary scientists, an age is a time in the past usually lasting millions of years. In contraposition, creationists use the term 'zone' to explain an ecological area that was matted together during or after the great flood and then floated away to burial or was buried *in situ*.

So, in summation, ancient earthers believe "index" fossils are representative of those fossils which are so common and supposedly unique to a given strata that it is alleged to enable them to identify the strata and the age of a geological layer, without even knowing anything else about it. To young-earth creationists, index fossils are something that evolutionists have deluded themselves into believing are useful for dating things, when in reality, they are only useful for determining the order of burial. This evolutionary thinking is nothing but pure circular reasoning at its worst. For creationists, I believe it is our duty to expose this false axiom to our fellow men with gentleness and respect (1 Peter 3:15). The truth is that index fossils were buried according to their ecology, topography and mobility. Furthermore, these so-called index fossils are sometimes found buried in layers where they should not be (according to evolutionary thinking). This phenomenon is unexplainable by evolutionary scientists.

Lastly, creationists believe the length of the flood was about five months and that it occurred about 4,300 years ago. Evolutionists believe that the earth and its creatures have been evolving for millions and billions of years. They specifically believe that the stratigraphic sequences were laid down between 5,000,000 to 1,500,000 years before present. Clearly one of these positions *must* be wrong. The Bible helps us to understand and should be depended upon for ultimate truth. Dependence on man's thinking is humanism and it cannot be reliable.

Endnotes

1. Humphreys, Russell; "Evidence for a Young World," Institute for Creation Research, 2005, http://www.icr.org/article/evidence-for-young-world/ (accessed September 1, 2011).

2. Ibid.

3. Ibid.

4. Sodera, Vij; *One Small Speck to Man*, (Malaysia, Vija Sodera Productions, 2009), 30.

5. Parker, Gary and Mary Parker; *The Fossil Book* (Green Forest, AR: Master Books, 2004), 10.

6. Sodera, Vij; *One Small Speck to Man*, (Malaysia, Vija Sodera Productions, 2009), 33.

7. Morris, John; *The Young Earth* (Green Forest, AR: Master Books, 2007), 74.

8. Parker, Gary and Mary Parker; *The Fossil Book* (Green Forest, AR: Master Books, 2004), 20-25.

9. Ibid.

CHAPTER 12

HISTORICAL AND ARCHAEOLOGICAL EVIDENCES

Written historic records only exist into the past about 4,000 to 5,000 years. This includes cave paintings, monuments and records of lunar phases.[1] Would intelligent man wait 185,000 to 190,000 years to begin recording his history (as supposed by evolutionists)? Absolutely not! In fact, the very thought that mankind would wait two thousand centuries to write things down is simply ludicrous.

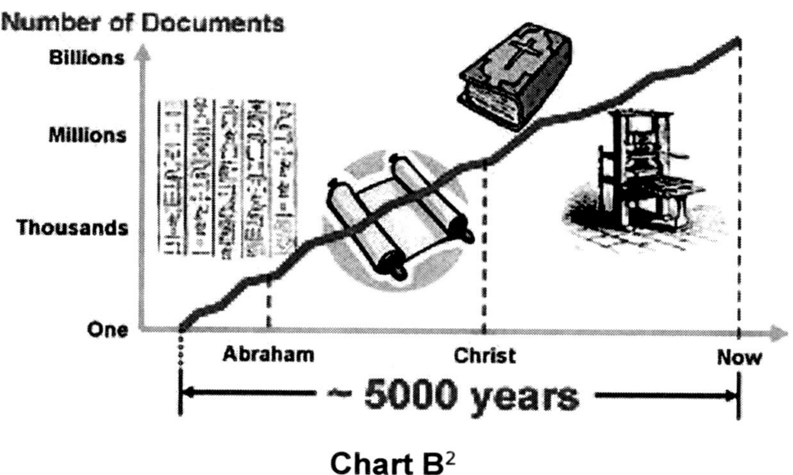

Chart B[2]

The truth is that men almost certainly knew how to write from the earliest of times. How can we know this? After all, did not Moses write the earliest known writings—the book of Genesis? There is no doubt that Moses edited the writings that made up the book of Genesis,[3] but he was not the originator of the base information itself.[4] The book of Genesis is actually a compilation of records from ancient authors including Adam, Seth, and others. How can we know this to be true?

The popular view is that Genesis was passed down by oral tradition, and that Moses copied it all down from the verbal memories of his ancestors and was hence, the originator of the first book of the Bible. However, the problem with that idea is that Genesis is not written in poetic form, which is the form necessary for lengthy memorization.[5] In fact, there are only two verses in the entire book of Genesis that follow the form of Hebrew poetry—Genesis 4:23-24. Additionally, an in-depth study and analysis of Genesis 1:1-2:3 was completed in 2005, and it was determined that there is a 99.5% probability (which is an extremely high level of confidence) that there is no poetry of any sort in the story of the creation.[6]

Another evidence that Moses did not originally write Genesis 1 includes the fact that the sun and the moon are not named in Chapter One. Instead, they are called lights.[7] However, later in Genesis, they are recognized as the sun and moon. If Moses had originated the section, he surely would have called them by the name common in his day so that everyone would recognize them as such. Another piece of evidence is that the chapters written before Abram's time contain roots of words that were used in Sumer, but the chapters written after Abram moved to Canaan (and sojourned in Egypt) include words from Canaan and Egypt.[8] If Moses had in fact written all of Genesis, then the entire style would have been based on his Egyptian learning.[9] The fact is that Moses took writings that he had available in his day and edited it with his own changes, which were all given by the inspiration of God Himself.

So, who did write Genesis? A good clue comes from the Bible itself. Consider the following passages:

> *This is the book of the generations of Adam.* Genesis 5:1a

This looks like a summation of the book of Adam at the end of his own writing. Then:

> *These are the generations of Noah.* Genesis 6:9a

That closed out Noah's section. We see this pattern throughout Genesis—where the faithful God-fearing men kept the records and genealogies of their families, generation after generation.

Additionally, there are very, very ancient stones, perhaps from shortly after the flood, near the mountains of Ararat with markings on them that cannot be understood.[10] Could it be a pre-Babel language or is it just so worn that it can't be made out? Another nearby stone has eight crosses on it. Could that represent the eight souls who were on the ark?[9] The locals call one of the nearby structures "*The House of Shem,*" and it has ancient inscriptions on it as well.[11]

In China, about 4,200 years ago, there lived God-fearing individuals who recorded their history in ideographs.[12] Ideographs combine 'radicals' or symbols to make words. In one example ideograph, the Chinese word for boat is a combination of three symbols: one for a vessel, one for the number eight, and one for people.[13] It seems like more than a strong coincidence that this probably originally represented the ark, Noah and his family (eight souls).

It is important to note, at this point, that the Bible is the only book of religious origin that specifies a beginning.[14] Furthermore, the Bible,

> "...declares that an eternal, omnipotent, omniscient, transcendent, and personal God created the entire universe."[15]

This means the Bible is the most trustworthy source for information about the beginnings that exists or has ever existed.

Archaeology

When it comes to digging up ancient artifacts, we find evidences of creation and a young earth everywhere. This is because God reveals truth to those who can see.

> *Truth shall spring out of the earth; and righteousness shall look down from heaven.* Psalm 85:11

However, it should be noted that archaeology in itself does not prove the Bible to be true; rather it confirms that it is true. What is the difference? Using archaeology (or any other discipline of knowledge) to prove the Bible requires one to place the authority of human findings above God's revealed Word—the Bible. If one pursues that way of thinking to the bitter end, one finds that the absolute determiner of truth would be defined by man, which is simply humanism. The reality is that archaeology, like every other area of scientific knowledge, must be treated as a secondary source and, therefore, subordinate to Scripture. Clifford Wilson explained it this way:

> "The Bible itself is the absolute; archaeology is not. If archaeology could prove the Bible, archaeology would be greater than the Bible, but it is not. The Bible comes with the authority of almighty God. It is His Word, and He is greater than all else."16

Nevertheless, archaeology is very relevant for understanding the Bible today.

Unfortunately, many of the dating methods used by archaeologists are not all that reliable. Some of these methods include ^{14}C dating, pollen analysis, pottery shapes[17] and by interpreting the layers in which the artifacts are buried. All these dating methods require additional witnesses in order to assure the said dating is accurate. Nevertheless, most secular scientists and many Christian archaeologists go ahead and interpret old ages, which are often in excess of 8,000 years, in spite of the fact that there is no direct evidence to support their belief. The most reliable dating of archaeological discoveries involves finding artifacts buried in layers along with written material[18] (usually on stone or clay) that includes dating authentication on the artifact itself or close by. The trustworthiness of these finds only goes back no further than 2400 B.C.[19] which is about 100 years earlier than our calculated limit for the Biblical flood. When one considers the error bars on archaeological dating, even these finds generally fall within the limits of the Biblical interpretation.

One of the problems with the archaeological system of interpretation (similar to the problems with the popular geological column idea) is that they name layers with such titles as "the Early Bronze Age" and state that it occurred between 3100 B.C. and 2000 B.C.[20] This might actually be possible if one included pre-flood artifacts in the mix. However, since the great flood disturbed the worldwide topography to such a great extent,[21] it seems very unlikely that this 'period' could have reliably included anything prior to 2300 B.C. Additionally, it is quite clear that brass (an alloy of copper and zinc) and iron were metals with which the earliest men were quite familiar with according to Genesis:

> *And Zillah, she also bare Tubalcain, an*

instructer of every artificer in brass and iron.
Genesis 4:22a

Bronze is an alloy of copper and tin. Iron is the most common element in the earth and is softer than aluminum, unless it is mixed with other elements. The trouble with extrapolating assumptions based on the commonality of findings of bronze in a given layer is that they soon evolve into permanent 'facts' by way of repeating the suppositions over and over, and then ultimately end up permanently inserted into textbooks as such. The result is a generation of students growing up believing that bronze was not even discovered until after such and such a year. Moreover, too many assumptions yield an outcome whereby archaeologists' presumptive claims will end up bringing their hypothetical "house" down like a deck of carefully-stacked playing cards set up in tower fashion (see image 'A') that have been blown over with a mere breath of air.

Image A[22]

In the end the reader should understand that the archaeological layers are somewhat arbitrarily named and dated based on a myriad of assumptions. Nevertheless, there are some Christian archaeologists who have properly interpreted the data for a more recent age of the earth, and have made great strides in understanding the dynasties of Egypt.

One recent example of this is John Ashton's and David Down's book, *Unwrapping the Pharaohs*. By using the Bible as their primary source, they were able to calculate a very plausible and perhaps correct view of the Egyptian Pharaoh lineage, which has troubled secular and Biblical scholars for many years. Ashton and Downs determined that the earliest pyramids in Egypt were built after the dispersion from Babel

(Genesis 11) and that the Egyptians continued to have trouble getting their bricks to line up perfectly, in order to complete a pyramid, until just about the time Abram would have showed up in Egypt, having traveled south from Haran and through Canaan. They explain that the ancient historian Josephus recorded that Abraham explained mathematics to the Egyptians[23] which enabled them to finally achieve the accuracy necessary to finish a pyramid—an example of which is in Khufu's pyramid.[24]

One of the interesting artifacts that has been discovered is the 'temptation seal' which is a cylindrical item that, when rolled out on something soft, such as wax, would leave an impression of a man, a woman holding out a piece of fruit, a tree, and a serpent.[25] The seal is dated around 4,300 years old[26] which correlates well with the flood date. Today, this artifact is located in the British Museum. This is a clear example of a representation of a real Biblical event—that of the temptation of Adam and Eve in the Garden of Eden. Another seal that resides in the British Museum is dated at 3300 B.C. It is clearly too old to fit the post-flood error bar. So, one must presume that either the date is wrong or it is an antediluvian artifact. This seal is that of an artists' rendering of an Apatosaurus—known today as a type of dinosaur.[27] Of course, that is another piece of evidence (of many) that dispels the myth that dinosaurs died out 65 million years ago, but that topic could fill an entire book, so we'll leave that issue alone for this chapter's purposes.

Another very interesting find is that of the Epic of Gilgamesh which includes nearly 200 lines of poetry about the global flood (a small part of the entire Epic which is 384 fragments of 12 clay tablets).[28] This secular and somewhat profane writing states that the

God who created man commanded a man by the name of Ut-napishtim to build a ship and to take all creatures with him.[29] Some of the facts in the poem do not match up with the Bible. For example, the dimensions of the ark are square rather than rectangular.[30] If we remember that only the Bible, not other documents, is inspired by God, we can use the Epic of Gilgamesh to fortify our faith in the Scripture because it does have some elements of truth in it, but the Epic itself should never be appealed to as an ultimate source of authority. The Epic of Gilgamesh dates around the 7th century B.C. However, it is a copy of earlier works[31] and was likely passed down from many years before.

Another endorsement of sorts comes from one of the great ungodly 'brains' of the past—that of the Greek philosopher Plato (b. 427 B.C. - d. 348 B.C.). Plato affirmed the historicity of the global flood in his writing, *The Laws*.[32] Also, lesser-known Sicilian historian, Diodorus Siculus (b. 90 B.C. - d. 21 B.C.), affirmed the beginning of time (creation).[33] Lastly, Josephus (b. 37 - d. 100), the secular Jewish historian, cited the truth of the Tower of Babel from Genesis Chapter 11.[34]

None of this chapter is meant to prove in the absolute sense that the earth is a few thousand years old; neither is it intended to provide an exhaustive list of all historical items in support of a young earth. However, it does provide a few definitive examples supporting an earth that is about 6,000 years old. When combined with other evidences and the Scripture, one can reach no other reasonable conclusion.

Endnotes

1. Humphreys, Russell; "Evidence for a Young World," Institute for Creation Research, 2005, retrieved from http://www.icr.org/article/evidence-for-young-world/ (accessed September 1, 2011).

2. Ibid.

3. Mortensen, Terry and Bodie Hodge; *Did Moses Write Genesis? How Do We Know the Bible is True?*, Ken Ham and Bodie Hodge, ed. (Green Forest, AR: Master Books, 2011), 94.

4. Beechick, Ruth; *Genesis: Finding Our Roots* (Pollock Pines, CA: Arrow Press, 1997), 29.

5. Ibid.

6. Vardiman, Larry, Andrew A. Snelling and Eugene E. Chaffin, ed.; *Radioisotopes and the Age of the Earth, vol. 2: The Results of a Young-Earth Creationist Initiative* (El Cajon, CA and Chino Valley AZ: Institute for Creation Research and Creation Research Society, 2005), 690.

7. Beechick, Ruth; *Genesis: Finding Our Roots* (Pollock Pines, CA: Arrow Press, 1997), 29.

8. Ibid.

9. Ibid.

10. Morris, John; *Noah's Ark and the Ararat Adventure* (Green Forest, AR: Master Books, 2001), 54.

11. Ibid., 55.

12. Nelson, Ethel R.; "The Chinese Language and the Creative Hands of God," Institute for Creation Research, 1987, http://www.icr.org/article/chinese-language-creative-hands-god/ (accessed September 9, 2011).

13. Kang, C.H. and Ethel R. Nelson; *The Discovery of Genesis* (St. Louis, MO: Concordia Publishing

House, 1979), 95.

14. Morris, Henry III; *The Big Three* (Green Forest, AR: Master Books, 2009), 100.

15. Ibid.

16. Wilson, Clifford; "Does Archaeology Support the Bible?," *The New Answers Book 1*, Ken Ham ed. (Green Forest, AR: Master Books, 2010), 322.

17. Wiseman, Donald J. and Edwin Yamauchi; *Archaeology and the Bible: An Introductory Study*, (Grand Rapids, MI: The Zondervan Corporation, 1979), 5-6.

18. Ibid., 5.

19. Ibid., 6,10.

20. Schoville, Keith N.; *Biblical Archaeology in Focus* (Grand Rapids, MI: Baker Book House Company, 1982), 36.

21. Parker, Gary; *Creation: Facts of Life* (Green Forest, AR: Master Books, 2006), 208.

22. Internet Image, http://thumbs.dreamstime.com/thumblarge_0/1088801721Kg3n32.jpg (accessed September 10, 2011).

23. Ashton, John and David Downs; *Unwrapping the Pharaohs* (Green Forest, AR: Master Books, 2006), 37.

24. Ibid.

25. Mitchell, T.C.; *The Bible in the British Museum* (Mahwah, NJ: Paulist Press, 2004), 24.

26. Ibid.

27. Gibbons, William J.; *Mokele-Mbembe: Mystery Beast of the Congo Basin* (Landisville, PA: Coachwhip Publications, 2010), 13.

28.Ceram, C.W.; *Gods, Graves, and Scholars* (New York: Vintage Books, 1979), 313-314.

29. Millard, Alan; *Treasures from Bible Times* (Oxford, England: Lion Publishing, 1985), 42.

30. Ibid.

31. Bluedorn, Harvey and Laurie Bluedorn; *Ancient History from Primary Sources*, (Muscatine, IA: Trivium Pursuit, 2003), 97.

32. Ibid., 153.

33. Ibid., 123.

34. Ibid., 142.

CHAPTER 13

A STUDY OF ASSUMPTIONS

"Scientists have **estimated** the age of the Earth at 4.6 billion years" [my emphasis in bold]. This ludicrous statement appears at the end of a section on radiocarbon dating, radioactive dating, radioactive decay and absolute dating of rocks in a recently-acquired, used high school science textbook.[1] It further states that carbon dating is useful up to 50,000 years and that uranium-lead dating is useful for dating rocks up to 4.5 billion years, and that these said ages are absolute.[2] How do they know this?

Interestingly, in the last paragraph of this same chapter, the statement is made that before radiometric dating was available, many people had estimated the age of the earth to be a few thousand years old. However, in the 1700s, a scientist by the name of James Hutton "**estimated** the age of the earth to be much older" [my emphasis in bold], through a model based on uniformitarianism. This model is one in which it is assumed that the earth's processes occurring today are similar to those that occurred in the past. Years later, Charles Lyell advanced the uniformitarian model substantially[3] and it has become accepted by a multitude of scientists and academia today. But how do they know that uniformitarianism is the best fit model?

Flash back to Chapter One of this same science textbook where the authors cited the definition of science. "Science is a process of observing and studying things in our world."[4] While this definition of science (really the scientific method) is a little light, it will suffice for the problem at hand. Since, by this definition, science must involve observation and no living person has ever been able to physically observe the long-ago past, then how do they know that uniformitarianism is true and that absolute ages of rocks are directly tied to the decay of radiogenic isotopes? Neither James Hutton, Charles Lyell, the authors of the cited textbook, their textbook consultants or their text reviewers could have possibly seen the occurrences of the unobserved past. Notice the careful use of the word "estimated" in paragraphs one and two above. Any sensible person must realize that estimation is not absolute, but it is pronounced to be "true" by the authors, who were science teachers with Master's degrees at the time of the writing. Do they know something we don't know? Could they have special insights because of their experience in teaching science? The book was also reviewed by science teachers, and the authors used nine consultants, several of whom possess terminal degrees in the sciences and in education. Does this mean they are more knowledgeable about the unseen past than the rest of us? Does their education make them super intelligent? Should we believe them because so many people endorsed the book?

While this chapter is not intended to be a book review, it is most useful to examine a couple of basic assumptions behind a high school science program. Why? Because the assumptions upon which this textbook are based are ultimately built upon a foundation of defective learning that these writers, teachers and scientists have "absorbed" within the cortex of their brains over time and these beliefs are no longer questioned.

The Age of the Earth

Amazingly, many high school textbooks do not seem to require references to support their writings, so apparently, we are to believe what is put before us as fact without question. We are to trust the authors, the reviewers, the consultants, the school boards and the state education agencies to verify their authenticity. However, most, if not all, college and university science textbooks have references listed in the back of the books or at the end of their chapters. One of the principal texts used in teaching radioisotope dating methodology at the university level is *Isotopes: Principles and Applications* by Gunter Faure and Teresa M. Mensing. On the very first page of the first chapter, the following statement is made: "...as time passed, geologists **accepted** the principle of Uniformitarianism"[5] [bold emphasis by me] and a little later on the same page, "...geologists **seemed very secure** in their conviction that the Earth was indeed very old and that long periods of time are required for the deposition of the great thickness of sedimentary rocks that had been mapped in the field"[6] [bold emphasis by me]. Note the phrase "*seemed very secure.*" This is a presupposition to which Faure clues the reader from the very beginning of his book. But where did he get it? Well, Faure cited Charles Lyell's book, *Principles of Geology,* to back up his assumption and he further backs it up with the plural "geologists" in the above quote. Faure apparently thinks that, because a number (perhaps a majority) of scientists believe that uniformitarianism is true, then it must be fact. This is a classical logical fallacy (see chapter 8). Another source that Faure cites is a book entitled *Lord Kelvin and the Age of the Earth* by J.D. Burchfield (1975) in which Kelvin (b. 1824 - d. 1907) came to the conclusion that the earth is much younger than billions of years. Burchfield concludes that Kelvin was wrong because he didn't have the information available then that is available to scientists today. Was this 'information' a new insight that enabled scientists to see the unobserved past? No! It was based on another assumption—the assumption that the radioactive materials released in the crust due to radiogenic decay are sufficient to significantly enhance the geothermal flux. Burchfield extrapolated this to interpret that the earth is in fact old.[7] But how can he really know?

In Chapter Nine of Faure's text, an explanation of a calculation via the neodymium-strontium radioisotope dating method is explained using what is commonly known as CHUR (chondritic uniform reservoir). Faure states that the CHUR value is derived from the dates obtained from stony meteorites, and yet he substitutes the "appropriate values" (of his own choosing) in the equation for a ratio of neodymium and defines the time 't' in the equation at 4.5 billion years. This is a classic example of circular reasoning, in other words—very bad logic (see Chapter 8). By this reasoning, the age of a sample using the ^{147}Sm-^{143}Nd method, is calculated using a predetermined age of the earth and the CHUR value (used in the calculation) is calculated based on the assumption that the earth is 4.5 billion years old. How can they know this is the fact?

Constancy of Decay Rates

There are many mathematical equations utilized in the sciences that use a number that is considered a constant, meaning that the scientist who developed said equation believed that such a number does not change and it is useful and trustworthy for calculating a myriad of conclusions related to that particular field of study. The science of radioisotope dating is built upon a foundation of assuming that the decay rate of each respective radioactive nuclide is in fact constant.[8] In fact, even in a recent upper elementary science textbook, the author cites a litany of 'facts' that are based upon this one assumption.[9] The author cites the use of uranium-lead dating by Claire Patterson, in 1953, to establish the age of the earth at approximately 4.5 billion years.[10] How ironic is it that the uniform half-life of ^{238}U just so happens to be about 4.5 billion years?[11]

The modern discovery of the process of radioactive decay occurred in 1902 when a pair of scientists, Rutherford and Soddy, studied the decay of ^{224}Ra. From this, the proportionality constant was defined as llamda (λ), also known as the decay constant, which fit into a calculus equation from which the currently used *model age equation* (applied to calculations for ages of rocks and minerals) was derived.[12] In a subsequent chapter of his book, Faure lists the four assumptions that must be accommodated in order for the results to be valid.[13] However, in most cases, none of the four assumptions are likely to be consistently valid (and three of them are likely rarely valid when dating samples older than a few thousand years). One of those assumptions is that the decay constant of the parent nuclide is known accurately and is not affected by external conditions to which it may be exposed.[14] Unfortunately, a great many scientists interpret these assumptions to be facts and build their studies, research, papers and academic careers upon this presuppositional foundation. How could they possibly know that these assumptions are, in fact, absolutely true?

The other assumptions include the presupposition that neither the parent nor the daughter nuclide concentrations have been altered throughout the entire history of the rock, that the original quantity of the daughter isotope is a known quantity and that measurements of the present values of the parent and daughter nuclides are accurate.[15] Interestingly, a number of rocks have been dated using the various radiogenic dating methods and it was discovered that many samples with *absolutely known* recent ages yielded ages in the millions of years.[16] Why is this discrepancy not reported in the 'important' scientific research journals?

Conclusion

Dr. Jobe Martin in *The Evolution of a Creationist* wrote,

> "The truth is that we have been taught a lie from our earliest school days".[17]

When children are taught that the assumptions are true and that the textbooks are not to be questioned, they learn in such a manner that they do not question said assumptions, nor do they question the mountain of assumptions that are built upon the original assumptions. Since many people do not know whom to trust, they end up placing their trust in what they perceive to be true (self-defined truth). Unfortunately, many believe the truth resides with whatever the majority of pedagogues and research scientists conclude. But they too are merely human, with a little more education and study in a certain field that was often taught with many underlying assumptions, including those cited earlier in this book, which were imbedded into their original educational curriculums, unbeknownst to them, as they progressed from elementary school to advanced degrees.

Why would a perfectly intelligent scientist or member of the academic world not question his own belief systems? Some do, but unfortunately, many never have and never will. This author suspects that much of the problem lies with the considerable amount of peer pressure that typically dooms anyone who dares to question the majority line of thinking. Also, since the secular evolutionists currently control most universities, state educational agencies and nationally recognized scientific journals, those who question the status quo are ostracized—specifically those who hold to a Biblical worldview and espouse the idea of a young earth and global deluge in recent history. Also, many academia and researchers have a vested interest in defending the "turf" upon which their papers, teachings and research are built.

Faure cited a myriad of references throughout his textbook, creating the illusion that his assumptions must have validity. However, while there is much good information in his and other science textbooks, the truth (according to his worldview) must reconcile with the observed and tested data, and it does not in many cases, because of the faulty assumptions. Additionally, it must agree with the data after being filtered through a Biblical worldview.

The idea of accelerated nuclear decay is a fairly new model that may explain away some of the past problems with dating layers of the geologic column. For example, the top layer of Grand Canyon has been dated at an older age than the bottom layer of Grand Canyon,[18] a serious problem for evolutionists. Dr. Steve Austin of the RATE team found that the decay rates of radioactive nuclides vary by their atomic weight and based on whether they are alpha emitters or beta emitters.[19] Could it be that the various radioactive parent elements were accelerated by some percentage based on similar principles at a time or times in the recent past? More research is needed on this important topic.

At the end of the day, the assumptions upon which scientists and everyone else infer their conclusions are based upon their worldview, whether they know it or not. Those who believe in uniformitarianism believe in evolution as a model and hence hold to a naturalistic worldview. Unfortunately for them, their model doesn't work very well. Those who believe in a God who created everything about 6,000 or so years ago hold to a purely Biblical worldview. The observed data fits the Biblical creationist model perfectly. The naturalists must continue to build on a "house of assumptions" in order to create some kind of thaumaturgy that does not involve a God of creation to support their delusion.

Endnotes

1. Feather, Ralph Jr. and Susan Leach Snyder; *Glencoe Earth Science* (Columbus, OH: Glencoe/McGraw Hill, 1999), 347.
2. Ibid., 346.
3. Ibid., 347.
4. Ibid., 6.
5. Faure, Gunter and Teresa Mensing; *Isotopes: Principles and Applications* (Hoboken, NJ: John Wiley and Sons, Inc., 2005), 3.
6. Ibid., 3-4.
7. Burchfield, J.D.; *Lord Kelvin and the Age of the Earth* (Chicago: University of Chicago Press, 1975).
8. Faure, Gunter and Teresa Mensing; *Isotopes: Principles and Applications* (Hoboken, NJ: John Wiley and Sons, Inc., 2005), 34, 53.
9. Victor, Edward and Richard D. Kellough; *Science for the Elementary and Middle School* (Upper Saddle River, NJ: Prentice-Hall, Inc., 1997), 587, 595.
10. Ibid., 296.
11. Faure, Gunter and Teresa Mensing; *Isotopes: Principles and Applications* (Hoboken, NJ: John Wiley and Sons, Inc., 2005), 216.
12. Ibid., 35.

13. Ibid., 57.

14. Ibid.

15. Ibid.

16. Morris, John; *The Young Earth* (Green Forest, AR: Master Books, 2007), 52.

17. Martin, Jobe; *The Evolution of a Creationist* (Rockwall, TX: Biblical Discipleship Publishers, 2004), 219.

18. Austin, Steve A.; *Grand Canyon: Monument to Catastrophe* (Santee, CA: Institute for Creation Research, 1994), 120-126.

19. Vardiman, Larry, Andrew A. Snelling and Eugene E. Chaffin, ed.; *Radioisotopes and the Age of the Earth, vol. 2: The Results of a Young-Earth Creationist Initiative* (El Cajon, CA and Chino Valley AZ: Institute for Creation Research and Creation Research Society, 2005), 385.

CHAPTER 14

FINAL THOUGHTS

The former Democratic mayor of New York, Ed Koch, recently said,

> ""I can't vote for a guy who says he can't believe in evolution..."[1]

One wonders how Koch can be so convinced that his information to support evolution is accurate? In a 2008 story from the Huffington Post, it was reported:

> "Soon after Sarah Palin was elected mayor of the foothill town of Wasilla, Alaska, she startled a local music teacher by insisting in casual conversation that men and dinosaurs coexisted on an Earth created 6,000 years ago—about 65 million years after scientists say most dinosaurs became extinct—the teacher said."[2]

Many of the posted on-line comments made fun of Palin for her view. Additionally, I observed very poor and ignorant arguments (mostly *ad hominem* attacks) to counter her viewpoint. This is fairly typical, from what I have observed, with regard to the proponents of evolution and a universe/earth that is believed to be billions of years old. This is principally because they do not have any arguments that are sufficiently strong to stand up to close scrutiny.

One reason for the heated on-line comments and for the refusal to listen to reason is explained in a book by Robert Chandler.

> "A high priority item for contemporary radical Leftists, therefore, is to destroy religion, a competitor for winning the "hearts and minds" necessary for Marxist revolution. For the Left,

> worship of God must be replaced by a worship of man, or "secular humanism.""[3]

He goes on to state that, for the ultra-Left, it is all about,

> "controlling the minds of the population."[4]

They have been somewhat successful in doing that when it comes to eradicating Christian-thinking, and family values, and re-educating persons from pre-K through the university level.[5] The Marxist view mirrors that of Antonio Gramsci's thinking. He wrote that the two driving tactics for replacing the Christian culture should be: (1) to repeat lies or half-truths over and over again until they are believed, and (2) to create new secular intellectuals by promoting anti-Christian thinking.[6] Chandler goes on to state of the new Marxists:

> "Their secular mentality will reject the Judeo-Christian theology of history and of man's origin and his end."[7]

So, this explains in very practical terms why it is so important to search for and to understand the truth. People simply cannot trust anything they read, hear, or see, with one single exception: the Holy Writ of God.

Satan perceives correctly that the Bible is one of the biggest obstacles blocking his imagined success for ensnaring the world. In the 1930s, a man by the name of Walter Grundmann was appointed by Adolf Hitler to serve as professor of New Testament studies at Jena University.[8] Grundmann tried to redefine Christianity by rewriting the New Testament in a book entitled *Die Botschaft Gottes* (The Message of God).[9] He removed all positive references to Judaism from the New Testament and wrote that Jesus was a warrior, not a servant or the meek lamb of God.[10] Over 200,000 copies were sold to the members of the liberal German church.[11] Do we see this sort of Bible revision going on today? No doubt! However, it looks a little bit different than it did back then.

Dr. James J.S. Johnson asks us to consider our real motive when defending the Bible and the derivative truths revealed therein:

> "Apologetics is more about honoring God than winning an argument. Scripturally speaking, the main purpose of apologetics is not to "win a case" like a litigator, because the "jury" may be hopelessly corrupt or distracted. Rather, apologetics is primarily a science for honoring the Lord by carefully studying and then accurately communicating His revealed truth (biblical, scientific, historical, etc.), especially those truths that are questioned or opposed or misrepresented, ultimately trusting God to accomplish His good with the truths communicated (Isaiah 55:10-11; Psalm 19:1-14; Romans 10:14-18). In other words, let God handle the results."[12]

Johnson also shares the story of some early American Unitarians (people who did not believe in the Biblical concept of the Divine Trinity) who fought with their Puritan 'brethren' over theology. In the end, the Puritans left the building and the furniture behind and moved on to start anew at another location. The Unitarians (unsaved nonbelievers) inherited the land, the building, and the furniture, but the Puritans kept their faith in God pure.[13] Which would you rather have: Finite furniture or infinite salvation?

I have spent very few words in this work in a direct refutation of the arguments of opponents of the young-earth view. This is partially because there is solid evidence supporting an approximately 6,000-

year-old universe, and I have an extremely high level of confidence in the facts, which grants me a level of security in my thinking to the point that I am not threatened by other belief systems. In fact, I welcome side-by-side comparisons, which in the end will only solidify my thinking. Some personify a near hysteria regarding the allowing of creationism to be taught anywhere near evolution. This, in itself, demonstrates a lack of security and a lack of confidence in my opponent's fact base.

This is not to say that I am incapable of refuting those who disagree, but that I chose not to spend many syllables to that end in this particular work. In point of fact, I believe that the ideas contained herein are defendable with a considerable amount of real evidence. That being said, I ask the reader to consider the cumulative value of the previous chapters. Even if you have trouble believing or understanding one particular concept or piece of evidence, perhaps you will find the totality of this work convincing. In the end, it is not me, but the Holy Spirit who allows one to see and understand things that involve the unseen, so I pray that you will look to Him for elucidation.

The Scriptures reveal the absolute truth; understanding that fact will get you everywhere. The first time and every time you question the Scripture in favor of man's thinking, you are enabling the devil's work. He is a master manipulator and not to be underestimated.

> *Be sober, be vigilant; because your adversary the devil, as a roaring lion, walketh about, seeking whom he may devour.* 1 Peter 5:8
>
> *He was a murderer from the beginning, and abode not in the truth, because there is no truth in him. When he speaketh a lie, he speaketh of*

his own: for he is a liar, and the father of it. John 8:44b

Perhaps you have read this book and are beginning to see the truth that God created the heavens and the earth about 6,000 years ago. If this is the case and you have never sought God previously, then now is the time to do that. If you have never repented and made a profession of faith and yet now see the truth, then thank the Holy Spirit for that, because God only reveals Himself to His chosen and He has been waiting patiently for you all along.

In order to be saved from eternal separation from God, you must first recognize and understand that you are a sinner.

For all have sinned, and come short of the glory of God. Romans 3:23

Second, you should repent, which means to turn away from sin and turn fully toward God.

I tell you, Nay: but, except ye repent, ye shall all likewise perish. Luke 13:3

What this verse does not mean is that you will never sin again. Saved Christians continue to struggle with sin, but have overcome its power by trusting in Christ. The third action you need to complete is to pray to God and tell Him in your own words that you believe Him and trust Him for all things.

For whosoever shall call upon the name of the Lord shall be saved. Romans 10:13

Then, thank God for saving you to Himself and for your eternal life. Thank Him for revealing Himself to you and for creating you. You can be absolutely assured of your salvation if, and only if, you truly appealed to God and trusted in God from your head and your heart and by realizing that God cannot lie.

So, when God says "*whosoever shall call upon the name of the Lord shall be saved,*" He really means it. That is not to say whosoever uses the Lord's name in vain or calls out the Lords name is saved, but whosoever believes Jesus was raised from the dead and trusts fully in Him.

This fact is clarified by:

> *Not every one that saith unto me, Lord, Lord, shall enter into the kingdom of heaven; but he that doeth the will of my Father which is in heaven.* Matthew 7:21

This verse is not a contradiction to Romans 10:13, but a verse in support of it. It helps us to understand that God wants the whole you—the heart and the mind—not just empty words. So, if we use words to call on the name of the Lord Jesus Christ, then we must mean it. And if we really mean it, we will demonstrate that true belief through our lives via our works. Consider James 2:17-26:

> *Even so faith, if it hath not works, is dead, being alone. Yea, a man may say, Thou hast faith, and I have works: shew me thy faith without thy works, and I will shew thee my faith by my works. Thou believest that there is one God; thou doest well: the devils also believe, and tremble. But wilt thou know, O vain man, that faith without works is dead? Was not Abraham our father justified by works, when he had offered Isaac his son upon the altar? Seest thou how faith wrought with his works, and by works was faith made perfect? And the scripture was fulfilled which saith, Abraham believed God, and it was imputed unto him for righteousness: and he was called the Friend of God. Ye see then how that by works a man is justified, and not by faith only. Likewise also was not Rahab the harlot justified by works,*

when she had received the messengers, and had sent them out another way? For as the body without the spirit is dead, so faith without works is dead also.

In other words, a true believer does the will of the Lord and a false believer does not.

What next? A true believer should want to know what his Redeemer and Creator expects of him *after* he is saved just as he needs to know how to be saved. God expects us to glorify Him in everything.

Let them praise the name of the Lord: for he commanded, and they were created. Psalm 148:5

The fact is that man is very, very special to God. God bent down and got His hands 'dirty' in the creation of man.

And the Lord God formed man of the dust of the ground, and breathed into his nostrils the breath of life; and man became a living soul. Genesis 2:7

And then when He made woman, he got his hands 'bloody' by opening Adam's side to acquire a rib and some flesh.

And the LORD God caused a deep sleep to fall upon Adam, and he slept: and he took one of his ribs, and closed up the flesh instead thereof; And the rib, which the LORD God had taken from man, made he a woman, and brought her unto the man. And Adam said, This is now bone of my bones, and flesh of my flesh: she shall be called Woman, because she was taken out of Man. Genesis 2:21-23

Our God is the God of the personal touch with regard to mankind. He didn't make the earth, plants or animals in this manner—only man and woman.

> *By the word of the LORD were the heavens made; and all the host of them by the breath of his mouth.* Psalm 33:6

> *I have made the earth, and created man upon it: I, even my hands, have stretched out the heavens, and all their host have I commanded.* Isaiah 45:12

So, God merely spoke (commanded) and breathed to make the universe. He could have done similarly with regard to man and woman, but He chose to add a personal touch to this special creation. Not only that, but God made man (and woman) in His own image.

> *And God said, Let us make man in our image, after our likeness.* ['us' and 'our' refers to the Trinity – God the father, God the Son, and God the Holy Spirit] Genesis 1:26a

So, knowing that we humans are made in God's image and that He personally touched us when creating us, it follows that we are all children of a King and not the progeny of monkeys or primordial soup as some might claim. However, each individual person can only claim that title as a child of the King by recognizing Him as such, and by trusting in Him absolutely.

As further evidence of man's specialness, consider this passage from Psalm 8:

> *When I consider thy heavens, the work of thy fingers, the moon and the stars, which thou hast ordained; What is man, that thou art mindful of him? and the son of man, that thou visitest him? For thou hast made him a little lower than the angels, and hast crowned him with glory and honour. Thou madest him to have dominion over the works of thy hands; thou hast put all things under his feet: All sheep and oxen, yea, and the beasts of the field; The*

> *fowl of the air, and the fish of the sea, and whatsoever passeth through the paths of the seas. O Lord our Lord, how excellent is thy name in all the earth!* Psalm 8:3-9

God has made us 'a little lower than the angels, and hast crowned [us] with glory and honour." Is that not incredible? It's definitely something to think about.

There have been a multitude of books written about creation, the flood and the truth of the Bible including Genesis 1-11. Most of them are lengthy or excessively technical or they have a primary agenda to refute some wrong thinking. This work is intended to be reasonably simple with a few dashes of technical jargon, and not too lengthy. However, I do have an agenda and that is to prove the age of the earth within a minimum and maximum range. Over the years, I have noticed that most people have no idea what the truth is with regard to this issue. So, I hope the reader has been edified in reading this work and will do further reading on the topic to solidify his or her thinking on the subject. Also, I hope you will share this work with others who are not so sure. I believe it is a popular topic and of great interest to most people. However, my real objective in writing this book is in hope that it might glorify God and that it might be used by the Holy Spirit to draw people to Himself, because this piece is really about Him and His creation—not about me or what I think.

τελέω

Endnotes

1. "Prominent Democrat threatens to dump Obama over Israel," World Net Daily, 2011, http://www.wnd.com/index.php?fa=PAGE.printable&pageId=346137 (accessed September 19, 2011).

2. Weiner, Rachel; "Palin Claimed Dinosaurs and People Coexisted," Huffington Post, 2008, http://www.huffingtonpost.com/2008/09/28/palin-claimed-dinosaurs-a_n_130012.html?view=print&comm_ref=false (accessed September 19, 2011).

3. Chandler, Robert; *Shadow World* (Washington, D.C.: Regnery Publishing, 2008), 29.

4. Ibid., 30.

5. Ibid., 38.

6. Ibid., 39.

7. Ibid.

8. Grigg, Russell; "Did Hitler Rewrite the Bible?," Creation magazine, vol. 33, no. 4 (Powder Springs, GA: Creation Ministries International, 2011), 14-17.

9. Ibid.

10. Ibid.

11. Ibid.

12. Johnson, James J.S.; "Understanding Effective Biblical Apologetics," Institute for Creation Research, 2010, http://www.icr.org/article/understanding-effective-biblical-apologetics/ (accessed September 25, 2011).

13. Johnson, James J.S.; "Fighting Over Furniture and Faith," Institute for Creation Research, 2010, http://www.icr.org/article/fighting-over-furniture-faith/ (accessed September 25, 2011).

APPENDIX

A BRIEF EXAMINATION OF THE UNREGENERACY OF WESTCOTT AND HORT AND OTHERS IN THE LINEAGE OF THE DOMINATE EDITORS, TRANSLATORS, AND COMPILERS WHO HAVE CONTRIBUTED SIGNIFICANTLY TO THE GREEK NEW TESTAMENT CRITICAL TEXT

Brian D. Shepherd

Master of Biblical Apologetics & Christian Education, Institute for Creation Research

37th Annual Dean Burgon Society Conference

Gatewood Baptist Church

4919 Gatewood Rd.

Garland, Texas 75043

July 22-23, 2015

Conservative and liberal theologians would most likely agree that few members of the general living population in the United States know much about the Greek language. Furthermore, most theologians would probably concur that the public is largely unaware that there are at least two main Greek text choices representing the foundation for a wide variety of New Testament versions. Most modern English versions have traceable roots to the 1881 Revised Version which was compiled by a committee of men dominated by Brooke Foss Westcott and Fenton John Anthony Hort and was largely founded on a Greek text of their own design.[1] These men and others in the lineage who have significantly influenced most modern Bible versions were almost certainly reprobate.[2] The evidence of their unregenerate hearts should lead modern conservative scholars and Biblical expositors to embrace a healthy suspicion of any works these men produced. Moreover, modern men should examine their own understanding of the best texts and seek direction from the Holy Spirit (1 Cor. 6:17, 19, Acts 7:51) before writing and speaking about the New Testament text for the purpose of influence lest the general populace be deceived in this or in future generations.

The roots of modern textual criticism can be traced to a liberal, German scholar by the name of Johann Jakob Griesbach (1745-1812).[3] Westcott and Hort borrowed much of their thinking from Griesbach's writings.[4] In fact, the late Kurt Aland, one of the principal editors for the Greek text most commonly used in seminaries today, claimed Griesbach's influence was significant (although he also believed it was somewhat exaggerated).[5] Modern scholars, Bruce Metzger and Bart Erhman have stated, "the importance of Griesbach for New Testament textual criticism can scarcely be overestimated."[6] It is also important to note that Hort built upon the original idea of Griesbach and his contemporary and mentor[7] Johann Salomo Semler, that there were three families of texts within the ancient Greek manuscripts (Hort decided there were four)[8] and a host of other illusory secular ideas without firm evidentiary support.

Griesbach studied under Semler in Halle (in what is geographically considered Germany today).[9] and at the University of Tubingen which was well known for its liberalism in the mid-1700s.[10] He would later join the University of Jena as a professor of New Testament studies.[11]

During his life, Griesbach visited archival collections in Europe for the purpose of collecting quotations of the Biblical Greek recorded by the patristics.[12] He also studied a few non-Greek translations of the New Testament including the Gothic, Armenian, and Philoxenian Syriac translations.[13] He believed that the manuscripts which were traceable to Alexandria, Egypt, could be sourced to Origen.[14]

Griesbach was a rationalist who did not believe in the plenary verbal inspiration of the Bible nor did he agree with many of the other important, foundational Biblical principles which are critical to good theology.[15] Furthermore, he never recorded any sort of personal salvation experience in any of his writings.[16] Griesbach wrote and published a critical style Greek New Testament text in 1796, which made its way to the United States in 1809 through Harvard's publishing of an American edition.[17] Among his most significant contributions to modern critical textual thinking were the establishment of the protocol and assumptions that were to be used by Westcott and Hort, and dominate, most likely, the method of almost all modern textual critics.[18]

His protocol which was influenced by Semler and others was comprised of 15 canons.[19]

The protocol was largely based on subjective thinking and humanistic principles of thinking from the ancient Greek secular rationalists such as Aristotle, Plato, and Socrates. The first canon included such statements as, "the shorter reading...is to be preferred" and "if the longer reading...seems to have come from lectionaries" and "the longer reading is to be preferred...if that which was omitted could have seemed to the scribe to be obscure, harsh, superfluous, unusual, paradoxical, offensive to pious ears, erroneous, or in opposition to parallel passages."[20] In other words, the final decision as to which textual variants were best was (and still is to modern textual critics) entirely arbitrary and subjective. Perhaps that explains why there are such a proliferation and variety of modern Bible versions.

Brooke Foss Westcott (1825-1901) graduated from Cambridge University in England during a time when the teaching there was very liberal and was completely unbiblical.[21] Over time, he moved up the ecclesiastical ladder and became the Bishop of Durham of the Church of England (Anglican with much Roman Catholic tradition and influence carried over from the past). One of his students, while he was still at Cambridge, was Fenton John Anthony Hort. In 1851, Westcott, along with Hort, began a long-term project to compile and publish a completely fresh Greek New Testament based on what they thought were the best available extant manuscripts of their day.[22] Semler's and Griesbach's writings significantly influenced Westcott and Hort during the thirty years they worked on the project.[23]

Westcott consistently questioned whether the Bible was literally true as demonstrated in this example from an entry in his diary from 1847: "I never read an account of a miracle but I seem instinctively to feel its improbability, and discover some want of evidence in the account of it."[24] It might seem strange that he had trouble believing in the supernatural in light of the fact that Westcott formed, along with Hort and others, a "Ghostlie Guild"[25] during his and Hort's work on the New Testament Greek. The purpose of this guild was to investigate supernatural appearances and their effects on things.[26] Hort confirmed this in an 1851 letter to the Reverend John Ellerton stating that the society believed that ghosts really do exist.[27] For two men so familiar with the Scripture, it seems incredulous that they would not have known the Biblical warnings about dabbling in the occult (Lev. 19:31, 20:6, Isa. 8:19, 19:3). Westcott and Hort denied the deity of Christ,[28] the inspiration of the Bible,[29] and Jesus Christ's vicarious atonement for all sinners by His crucifixion and resurrection.[30] They also held the view that Jesus atoned for the sins of the many by way of His conception through Mary and by His birth,[31] which led to their worship of Mary. In fact, in 1865, Westcott wrote to Archbishop Benson: "I wish I could see to what forgotten truth Mariolatry bears witness."[32] Hort confirmed that he likewise venerated Mary in a letter to the Reverend Rowland Williams in the same year by stating, "I have been persuaded for many years that Mary-worship and 'Jesus-worship' have very much in common in their causes and their results."[33]

Another evidence of Westcott's heresy is found in a commentary he wrote on the gospel of John regarding John 1:29, "the parallel passage in the Epistle (l.c.) shews that the REDEMPTIVE EFFICACY OF CHRIST'S WORK is to be found IN HIS WHOLE LIFE (He was manifested) crowned by His Death."[34] Westcott attempted to build a case for Christ's life being what saves sinners, not His death and resurrection, which is totally incorrect soteriological reasoning. Moreover, Westcott denied the pre-existence of God,[35] and he denied the deity of Christ[36] in multiple writings. There are many other letters and articles on Bishop Westcott, which lead to an irrefutable conclusion that he was not regenerated to salvation.

Professor Hort (1828-1892) worked closely with Westcott under whom he studied while at Cambridge, to produce the new Greek text based largely on the corrupt[37] *Codex Vaticanus,* and to produce what was called the English Revised Version, in 1881. During the time they worked on *The New Testament in the Original Greek,* they were also both members of the "Ghostlie Guild." This in itself is very good evidence that they were not guided in any form or fashion by the Holy Spirit while studying and working on what ultimately became transformed (through many revisions) into the modern Greek text produced by the United Bible Societies which is used today for translating Bibles into languages all over the world. In fact, they may very well have been demon-guided.

Hort and Westcott were both committed evolutionists.[38] Hort wrote in a letter to John Ellerton in 1860 that "the book which has most engaged me is Darwin. Whatever maybe thought of it, it is a book that one is proud to be contemporary with. ...My feeling is strong that the theory [of evolution] is unanswerable."[39] Hort also wrote in *The New Testament in the Original Greek*, that he and Westcott "revered the name of Griesbach 'above that of every other textual critic of the New Testament'."[40]

In 1858, Hort wrote in a letter to Reverend Rowland Williams that "the positive doctrines even of the Evangelicals seem to me perverted rather than untrue. There are I fear, still more serious differences between us on the subject of authority, and especially the authority of the Bible."[41] Furthermore, Hort affirmed his belief that priests, by way of having been ordained into the priesthood, acquired supernatural powers.[42] He did not believe in the priesthood of the believer and called it a "crazy horror."[43] Hort wrote another letter to Reverend John Ellerton in 1846 in which he said, "the pure Romish view seems to me nearer, and more likely to lead to, the truth than the evangelical view. ...We dare not forsake the sacraments or God will forsake us."[44]

In another example, Hort wrote to his friend Westcott in 1861 that he preferred Greek philosophy and its "precious truth" to the Christian revelation [the Bible] in which he said he found nothing and that he did not expect to find anything.[45]

Lastly, Hort wrote these words to Westcott on October 15, 1860, leaving little doubt that he was unsaved:

To-day's post brought also your letter to the Eggischhorn, which I should have been very sorry to have missed. I entirely agree----correctly one word---- with what you there say on the Atonement having for many years believed that "the absolute union of the Christian (or rather, of man) with Christ Himself" is the spiritual truth of which the popular doctrine of substitution is an immoral and material counterfeit. But I doubt whether that answers the question as to the nature of the satisfaction. Certainly nothing can be more unscriptural than the modern limiting of Christ's bearing our sins and sufferings to His death; but indeed that is only one aspect of an almost universal heresay.[46]

These are but a few examples of many that

demonstrate to the careful reader that Professor Hort was anything but regenerated. The Scripture records that just because someone calls upon the name of the Lord does not necessarily mean that he will be saved (Matt. 7:21). Salvation requires believing and trusting in the Christ (John 11:26, Eph. 1:13).

Through the years, there have appeared to be four common principles shared by most of those textual critics who emphatically embrace the Westcott-Hort version of the New Testament in Greek (and by default the modern Nestle-Aland [United Bible Societies] version since it is itself founded on the Westcott-Hort work). First, they seem to revere Origen (AD 185-254) as the best source for truth with regard to compilation of ancient witnesses. Second, they believe that the *Codex Vaticanus* is the "oldest and best" ancient text without regard for the volumetric evidence against it. Third, they place man's thinking above God's omniscience in determining truth, which might rightly be called religious humanism. Fourth, none of the key leaders who, through the years, have passionately propagated, edited, and refined what has become popularly known as the Critical Text seem to be regenerate.[47]

Origen, a third century headmaster of the seminary in Alexandria, Egypt, was a Gnostic[48] who knew how to play politics. He wrote some sound exegesis as well as some scripturally untenable expositions that clearly identify him as an unregenerate apostate. For example, he was a universalist, he did not believe in the resurrection of the body, and he even taught that infant baptism led to forgiveness of sins.[49] He took Matthew 5:29-30 somewhat literally and had himself castrated.[50] This could not possibly have been the reaction of a man who had been led by the Holy Spirit. It seems clear that he was being demon-led, especially when one considers the cumulative errors in his writing with regard to Scriptural hermeneutics.

Modern Bible scholar Daniel B. Wallace, professor at Dallas Theological Seminary, touted some of his heroes in an interview in 2006. Among his favorites were Origen, Hort, Bruce Metzger, and Bart Erhman, along with a number of other apostate individuals.[51] Metzger, who died in 2007, was a professor at Princeton Theological Seminary for many years. Princeton drifted to liberalism in 1929[52] and it has never recovered. Metzger did not accept the inspiration and inerrancy of Scripture. He also believed that many of the stories in the Bible are mythological or allegorical.[53] Together with Bart Erhman, a self-admitted agnostic and professor of religion at the University of North Carolina, Metzger co-wrote a book entitled *The Text of the New Testament* which is popular in seminaries and used by pastors around the country.

Professor Wallace summed up their way of thinking when he said in the same interview mentioned previously that he "found himself agreeing more and more with reasoned eclecticism."[54] Reasoned eclecticism is nothing more than religious humanism dressed up with a fancy title. It assumes that the educated scholar is the most able to choose the best text variants from all of the ancient, extant manuscripts, using his allegedly, superior knowledge. It eliminates the Holy Spirit from the method. Ultimately, it takes man's reason and uses it to trump God.

Conclusion

Modern theologians, scholars, and pastors should pay careful heed to the inspired wisdom shared by the apostle Peter: *"be sober, be vigilant; because your adversary the devil, as a roaring lion, walketh about, seeking whom he may devour"* (1 Pet. 5:8). Many godly men have been caught up with their sense of self-importance by way of having been published and by their advanced degrees. The prophet Jeremiah warned Judah, "the heart is deceitful above all things, and desperately wicked: who can know it" (Jer. 17:9)? How easy it has been over the years to be swayed by the liberal way of thinking, yet the conservative theologian would be wise to consider that the true liberals will almost certainly have no part in paradise in the end. Perhaps the modern human emphasis on grace has even been overdone to the sacrifice of truth. Not that grace is unimportant. God's grace to salvation is the reason that saved men pursue righteousness and good works. However, there should be a limit on the amount of grace granted to the unsaved by believing men, because *"there is a way which seemeth right unto a man, but the end thereof are the ways of death"* (Prov. 14:12). Men should stand firm for the truth in love above all else (1 Cor. 13:6, 16:13, Eph. 6:14).

Also, scholars should be wary of the devil and yet, be respectful of him as the archangel Michael demonstrated by example in the book of Jude. He rebuked the devil in the name of the Lord, not through his own wisdom. Surely Michael's wisdom is wiser than men's wisdom, yet many men think they are wiser because of their study of humanistic thinking in the sciences, history, and literature.

The educated lineage of key leaders who have cried the loudest for the Critical Text supporting most modern English versions of the Bible were chiefly reprobate. To be sure, they were popular, respected, and even revered in many cases. They may have even been nice people, but the Bible has nothing to say about truth being equal with niceness. In fact, it is often the opposite. The prophets often dished out harsh messages. Jesus often criticized the religious leaders (probably the most educated of their day) for being like serpents and vipers, and even had some sharp words for his disciples on occasion. The apostles wrote very pointed messages about avoiding all appearances of evil and about the need to be influenced by only good things. Perhaps it is time for many modern scholars and leaders to step back in humility and to search the true, inspired, and inerrant Scriptures for absolute truth as God Himself directs, rather than by their own deceitful hearts and by private interpretation (2 Pet. 1:20). The Critical Text has failed to measure up. It seems, more likely, that the truest preserved text (1 Pet. 1:23, 25, Matt. 24:35, John 10:35, Isa. 40:9) may be found in the *Textus Receptus* which is more credibly the best New Testament text. The apostle Paul admonished the believers in Thessalonica to "prove all things" (1 Thess. 5:21) and that was a message that is well suited for all believers today especially when deciding which Greek text is best for making life's most important decisions.

Endnotes

1. Moorman, Jack; *Forever Settled: A Survey of the Documents and History of the Bible* (Collingswood, NJ: The Dean Burgon Society, 2009), 271.

2. Sorenson, David H.; *God's Perfect Book: The Inspiration, Preservation, and Alteration of the Bible* (Duluth, MN: Northstar Ministries, 2009), 113.

3. Metzger, Bruce M. and Bart D. Erhman; *The Text of the New Testament: Its Transmission,*

Corruption, and Restoration, 4th ed. (New York: Oxford University Press, 2005), 165.

4. Fuller, David Otis, ed.; *True or False? The Westcott-Hort Textual Theory Examined* (Grand Rapids: Grand Rapids International Publications, 1990), 218.

5. Aland, Kurt and Barbara Aland; *The Text of the New Testament: An Introduction to the Critical Editions and to the Theory and Practice of Modern Textual Criticism,* 2nd ed., trans. Erroll F. Rhodes (Grand Rapids: William B. Eerdmans Publishing Company, 1995), 9.

6. Metzger and Erhman, *The Text of the New Testament*, 167.

7. Sorenson, *God's Perfect Book*, 102.

8. Jones, Floyd Nolen; *Which Version is the Bible?* 19th ed., (Goodyear, AZ: KingsWord Press, 2006), 122.

9. Metzger and Erhman, *The Text of the New Testament*, 165.

10. Sorenson, *God's Perfect Book*, 102.

11. Metzger and Erhman, *The Text of the New Testament*, 165.

12. Ibid.

13. Ibid.

14. Ibid.

15. Sorenson, *God's Perfect Book*, 102.

16. Ibid., 102-103.

17. Ibid., 102.

18. Ibid.

19. Metzger and Erhman, *The Text of the New Testament*, 166.

20. Ibid.

21. Sorenson, *Touch Not the Unclean Thing*, 16

22. Ibid.

23. Sorenson, *God's Perfect Book*, 105.

24. Westcott, Brooke Foss and Arthur Westcott; *Life and Letters of Brooke Foss Westcott, D.D., D.C.L.: Sometime Bishop of Durham, vol. 1* (London: MacMillan and Co., 1903), 52.

25. Ibid., 117.

26. Ibid., 117.

27. Hort, Fenton John Anthony and Arthur Hort; *Life and Letters of Fenton John Anthony Hort, D.D., D.C.L., LL.D., Sometime Hulsean Professor and Lady Margaret's Reader in Divinity in the University of Cambridge, vol. 1* (London: MacMillan and Co., 1896), 211.

28. Jones, *Which Version is the Bible?*, 60

29. Ibid.

30. Ibid., 58.

31. Ibid.

32. Westcott and Westcott, *Life and Letters of Brooke Foss Westcott, vol. 1*, 81.

33. Hort, Fenton John Anthony and Arthur Hort; *Life and Letters of Fenton John Anthony Hort, D.D., D.C.L., LL.D., Sometime Hulsean Professor and Lady Margaret's Reader in Divinity in the University of Cambridge, vol. 2* (London: MacMillan and Co. 1896), 50.

34. Waite, Donald A.; *Heresies of Westcott and Hort (As Seen in Their Own Writings)*, Rev. ed. (Collingswood, NJ: The Bible for Today Press, 2004), 25. The emphasis (capitalization) is D.A. Waite's and quoted exactly as he did in his book.

35. Ibid., 29.

36. Ibid., 31.

37. Metzger and Erhman, *The Text of the New Testament*, 322.

38. Jones, *Which Version is the Bible?*, 58

39. Hort and Hort, *Life and Letters of Fenton John Anthony Hort, vol. 1*, 416.

40. Sorenson, *God's Perfect Book*, 105.

41. Hort and Hort, *Life and Letters of Fenton John Anthony Hort, vol. 1*, 400.

42. Hort and Hort, *Life and Letters of Fenton John Anthony Hort, vol. 2*, 86.

43. Ibid., 51.

44. Hort and Hort, *Life and Letters of Fenton John Anthony Hort, vol. 1*, 76-77.

45. Ibid., 449.

46. Ibid., 430.

47. Sorenson, *God's Perfect Book*, 113.

48. Ibid., 151.

49. Ibid., 152.

50. Jones, *Which Version is the Bible?*, 27.

51. Williams, P.J.; "Interview with Dan Wallace." Evangelical Textual Criticism Blog, entry posted March 20, 2006, http://evangelicaltextualcriticism.blogspot.com/2006/03/ interview-with-dan-wallace.html [accessed June 2, 2012].

52. Jones, *Which Version is the Bible?*, 40.

53. Sorenson, *God's Perfect Book*, 113.

54. Williams, P.J.; "Interview with Dan Wallace."

BIBLIOGRAPHY

Adams, S.C. *Adams Synchronological Chart*. Green Forest, AR: Master Books, 2007.

Aland, Kurt, and Barbara Aland. *The Text of the New Testament: An Introduction to the Critical Editions and to the Theory and Practice of Modern Textual Criticism.* 2nd ed. Translated by Erroll F. Rhodes. Grand Rapids: William B. Eerdmans Publishing Company, 1995.

Ashton, John F., ed. *In Six Days: Why Fifty Scientists choose to Believe in Creation*. Green Forest, AR: Master Books, 2003.

Ashton, John, and David Downs. *Unwrapping the Pharaohs*, Green Forest, AR: Master Books, 2006.

Austin, Steve A. *Grand Canyon: Monument to Catastrophe*. Santee, CA: Institute for Creation Research, 1994.

Beale, David O. *In Pursuit of Purity*. Greenville, SC: Unusual Publications, 1986.

Beechick, Ruth. *Genesis: Finding our Roots*. Pollock Pines, CA: Arrow Press, 1997.

Bennett, David C. *God's Marvelous Book—The Bible*. Collingswood, NJ: The Bible for Today Press, 2013.

------. *Dean John Burgon's Defense of the Authorized Version*. Collingswood, NJ: The Bible for Today Press, 2014.

Bergman, Jerry. *Slaughter of the Dissidents*. Southworth, WA: Leafcutter Press, 2008.

Bluedorn, Harvey, and Laurie Bluedorn. *Ancient History from Primary Sources*. Muscatine, IA: Trivium

Pursuit, 2003.

Boettner, Loraine. *Roman Catholicism*. Grand Rapids, MI: Baker Book House, 1980.

Bowden, M. *Ape-Men – Fact or Fallacy? A Critical Examination of the Evidence*. Bromley, Kent, England: Sovereign Publications, 1977.

Burchfield, J.D. *Lord Kelvin and the Age of the Earth*. Chicago: University of Chicago Press, 1975.

Burgon, John W. *The Causes of Corruption of the New Testament Text*. LaFayette, IN: Sovereign Grace Publishers, 1998.

------. *Inspiration and Interpretation*. Collingswood, NJ: Dean Burgon Society Press, 1999.

------. *The Last Twelve Verse of Mark Vindicated Against Recent Critical Objectors & Established*. Collingswood, NJ: Dean Burgon Society Press, 2002.

------. *The Revision Revised: A Refutation of Westcott and Hort's False Greek Text and Theory*. Collingswood, NJ: Dean Burgon Society, 2000.

Ceram, C.W. *Gods, Graves, and Scholars*. New York: Vintage Books, 1979.

Chandler, Robert. *Shadow World*. Washington, D.C.: Regnery Publishing, 2008.

Chiniquy, Charles. *50 Years in the Church of Rome: The Conversion of a Roman Catholic Priest.* Ontario, CA: Chick Publications, 1985.

Chittick, Donald E. *The Puzzle of Ancient Man*. Newberg, OR: Creation Compass, 2006.

Clark, Gordon. *Logic*. Unicoi, TN: The Trinity Foundation, 2004.

------. Logical Criticisms of Textual Criticism.

Jefferson, MD: The Trinity Foundation, 1990.

Cloud, David. *The Bible Version Issue*. Port Huron, MI: Way of Life Literature, 2006.

------. *The Bible Version Question/Answer Database: Answering the Myths Promoted by Modern Version Defenders*. Port Huron, MI: Way of Life Literature, 2005.

------. *Genesis*. Port Huron, MI: Way of Life Literature, 2004.

------. *The Mobile Phone and the Christian Home and Church*. Port Huron, MI: Way of Life Literature, 2016.

------. *The Modern Version Hall of Shame*. Port Huron, MI: Way of Life Literature, 2009.

Collingsworth, Gerald B. *Prove It!* Mogadore Village, OH: Gerald B. Collingsworth, 1995.

Cooper, William. *After the Flood*. West Sussex, England: New Wine Press, 1995.

------. *The Authenticity of the Book of Genesis*. England: The Creation Science Movement, 2011.

------, *The Forging of Codex Sinaiticus*. England: Kindle edition, 2016.

Creation Basics and Beyond. An In-Depth Look at Science, Origins, and Evolution. Dallas, TX: Institute for Creation Research, 2013.

Cummings, Violet M. *Noah's Ark: Fable or Fact?* San Diego, CA: Creation-Science Research Center, 1973.

Cuozzo, Jack. *Buried Alive: The Startling Untold Story About Neanderthal Man*. Green River, AR: Master Books, 1998.

Daniels, David W. *Why They Changed the Bible*. Ontario, CA: Chick Publications, 2016.

Denny, Edward. *Forgiveness Seventy and Sevenfold, Companion to Two Prophetical Charts*. London: James Nisbet and Co., 1849.

Down, David. *The Archaeology Book*. Green Forest, AR: Master Books, 2010.

Edwards, Brian. Nothing But the Truth. Faverdale North, Darlington, England: Evangelical Press, 2006.

Faure, Gunter, and Teresa Mensing. *Isotopes: Principles and Applications*. Hoboken, NJ: John Wiley and Sons, Inc., 2005.

Feather, Ralph, Jr., and Susan Leach Snyder. *Glencoe Earth Science*. Columbus, OH: Glencoe/McGraw Hill, 1999.

Ferrell, Vance. *The Evolution Handbook*. Altamont, TN: Evolutions Facts, Inc., 2005.

Fox, John. *Fox's Book of Martyrs*. Grand Rapids, MI: Zondervan, 1954.

Fuller, David Otis, ed. *Counterfeit or Genuine: Mark 16? John 8?* Grand Rapids, MI: Grand Rapids International Publications, 1978.

------. *True or False? The Westcott-Hort Textual Theory Examined*. Grand Rapids: Grand Rapids International Publications, 1990.

------. *Which Bible?* Grand Rapids: Grand Rapids International Publications, 1990.

Gibbons, William J. *Mokele-Mbembe: Mystery Beast of the Congo Basin*. Landisville, PA: Coachwhip Publications, 2010.

Gilley, Gary E. *This Little Church Stayed Home*. Darlington, England: Evangelical Press, 2008.

Gish, Duane T. *Evolution: The Fossils Still say NO!* El Cajon, CA: Institute for Creation Research, 2006.

Grant, George. *Killer Angel*. Nashville, TN: Cumberland House Publishing, 2001.

Griesbach, Johann Jakob. *The New Testament in the Common Version: Conformed to Griesbach's Standard Greek Text*. Edited by John Gorham Palfrey. Boston: Gray and Bowen, 1830.

Ham, Ken, ed., *The New Answers Book 1*. Green Forest, AR: Master Books, 2010.

Ham, Ken and Britt Beemer. *Already Gone*. Green Forest, AR: Master Books, 2009.

Hannam, James. *The Genesis of Science*. Washington, DC: Regnery Publishing, Inc., 2011.

Harris, J. Rendel. *Stichometry*. London: C.J. Clay and Sons, 1893.

Helfinstine, Robert F., and Jerry D. Roth. *Texas Tracks and Artifacts: Do Texas Fossils Indicate Coexistence of Men and Dinosaurs?* Anoka, MN: R & J Publishing, 2007.

Hills, Edward F. *Believing Bible Study*. Des Moines, IA: The Christian Research Press, 1991.

------. *The King James Bible Defended*. Des Moines, IA: The Christian Research Press, Ltd., 2006.

Hislop, Alexander. The Two Babylons. Neptune, NJ: Loizeaux Brothers, 1959.

Hoerth, Alfred J. *Archaeology and the Old Testament*. Grand Rapids, MI: Baker Publishing Group, 2007.

Hort, Fenton John Anthony, and Arthur Hort. *Life and Letters of Fenton John Anthony Hort, D.D., D.C.L., LL.D.,: Sometime Hulsean Professor and Lady*

Margaret's Reader in Divinity in the University of Cambridge, vol. 1. London: MacMillan and Co., 1896.

------. *Life and Letters of Fenton John Anthony Hort, D.D., D.C.L., LL.D., Sometime Hulsean Professor and Lady Margaret's Reader in Divinity in the University of Cambridge, vol. 2*. London: MacMillan and Co., 1896.

Iserbyt, Charlotte Thomson. *The Deliberate Dumbing Down of America.* Athens, GA: The Athens Printing Company, 2001.

Jones, Floyd Nolen. *The Chronology of the Old Testament*. Green Forest, AR: Master Books, 2009.

------. Ripped out of the Bible. Goodyear, AZ: Word of God Publishing, 2004.

------. *The Septuagint: A Critical Analysis*. The Woodlands, TX: KingsWord Press, 2000.

------. *Which Version is the Bible?* 19th ed. Goodyear, AZ: KingsWord Press, 2006.

Jones, Rick. *Understanding Roman Catholicism*. Ontario, CA: Chick Publications, 1995.

Jurgens, William A., trans. *The Faith of the Early Fathers.* Collegeville, MN: The Liturgical Press, 1970.

Kang, C.H., and Ethel R. Nelson. *The Discovery of Genesis: How the Truths of Genesis were Found Hidden in the Chinese Language*. St. Louis, MO: Concordia Publishing House, 1979.

Kerr, William Shaw. *A Handbook on the Papacy*. New York: Philosophical Library, Inc., 1951.

Kriessman, Charles. *Modern Version Failures*. Collingswood, NJ: The Bible for Today Press, 2014.

Kroll, Woodrow. *Taking Back the Good Book*. Wheaton, IL: Crossway Books, 2007.

Kulus, Chester W. *One Tittle Shall in No Wise Pass*. Cleveland, GA: The Old Paths Publications, 2009.

Kupelian, David. *The Marketing of Evil*. Los Angeles: WND Books, 2005.

Lawrence, Debbie, and Richard Lawrence. *God's Design for Heaven and Earth: Our Universe*. Windsor, CO: R and D Publishing Center, LLC, 2003.

Lewis, C.S. *Mere Christianity*. Indianapolis, IN: Collier Publishing, 1960.

Lindsell, Harold. *The Battle for the Bible*. Grand Rapids, MI: The Zondervan Corporation, 1976.

Lisle, Jason. *Taking Back Astronomy*. Green Forest, AR: Master Books, 2007.

------. *The Ultimate Proof of Creation*. Green Forest, AR: Master Books, 2009.

Lloyd-Jones, D.M. *What is an Evangelical*. Edinburgh, England: The Banner of Truth Trust, 1992.

Martin, Charles. *Flood Legends*. Green Forest, AR: Masters Books, 2009.

Martin, Jobe. *The Evolution of a Creationist*. Rockwall, TX: Biblical Discipleship Publishers, 2004.

Martin, Malachi. *The Jesuits*. New York: Simon and Schuster, 1987.

McDurmon, Joel. *Biblical Logic in Theory and Practice*. Powder Springs, GA: The American Vision, 2009.

McKendrick, Scot, David Parker, Amy Myshrall, and Cillian O'Hogan, ed. Codex Sinaiticus: *New Perspectives on the Ancient Biblical Manuscript*. London: The British Library, 2015.

Merrill, Eugene. *An Historical Survey of the Old*

Testament. Grand Rapids, MI: Baker Books, 2009.

Metzger, Bruce. *The New Testament: Its Background, Growth, and Content*, 3rd ed. Nashville, TN: Abingdon Press, 2003.

Metzger, Bruce M., and Bart D. Erhman. *The Text of the New Testament: Its Transmission, Corruption, and Restoration*. 4th ed. New York: Oxford University Press, 2005.

Millard, Alan. *Treasures from Bible Times*. Oxford, England: Lion Publishing, 1985.

Miller, Edward. *The Oxford Debate on the Textual Criticism of the New Testament*. Edited by H.D. Williams. Cleveland, GA: The Old Paths Publications, 2009.

------. *A Guide to Textual Criticism of the New Testament*. Collingswood, NJ: The Dean Burgon Society, 2003.

Mitchell, T.C. *The Bible in the British Museum*. Mahwah, NJ: Paulist Press, 2004.

Moorman, Jack. *Bible Chronology, the Two Great Divides: A Defense of the Unbroken Biblical Chronology from Adam to Christ*. Cleveland, GA: The Old Paths Publications, 2010.

------. *Early Manuscripts, Church Fathers, and the Authorized Version*. Collingswood, NJ: The Bible for Today Press, 2005.

------. *Forever Settled: A Survey of the Documents and History of the Bible*. Collingswood, NJ: The Dean Burgon Society, 1999.

------. *Missing in Modern Bibles: The Old Heresy Revived*. Cleveland, GA: The Old Paths Publications, 2009.

------. *Over 8,000 Differences Between the N.T. Greek Words of the King James Bible and the Modern Versions*. Collingswood, NJ: The Bible for Today Press and the Dean Burgon Society (jointing printing), 2006.

------. *Samuel P. Tregelles*. Collingswood, NJ: The Bible for Today Press, 2004.

------. *When the KJV Departs from the "Majority" Text*. Collingswood, NJ: Dean Burgon Society Press, 2010.

Morris, Henry. *The Genesis Flood: The Biblical Record and its Scientific Implications*. Phillipsburg, NJ: R & R Publishing, 2003.

------. The Genesis Record: A Scientific and Devotional Commentary on the Book of Beginnings. Grand Rapids, MI: Baker Book House, 1976.

------. *The Long War Against God: The History and Impact of the Creation/Evolution Conflict*. Green River, AR: Master Books, 2000.

------. *That Their Words May Be Used Against Them*. Green Forest, AR: Master Books, 2000.

Morris III, Henry. *The Big Three*. Green Forest, AR: Master Books, 2009.

Morris, Henry M., and John D. Morris. *The Modern Creation Trilogy*. Green Forest, AR: Master Books, 1996.

Morris, John. *Is the Big Bang Biblical?* Green Forest, AR: Master Books, 2004.

Morris, John. *Noah's Ark and the Ararat Adventure*. Green Forest, AR: Master Books, 2001.

------. *The Young Earth*. Green Forest, AR: Master Books, 2007.

Morris, John, and Steve Austin. *Footprints in the*

Ash. Green Forest, AR: Master Books, 2005.

Morris, John, and Frank J. Sherwin. *The Fossil Record*. Dallas, TX: Institute for Creation Research, 2010.

Mortensen, Terry, and Bodie Hodge. *Did Moses Write Genesis? How Do We Know the Bible is True?* Green Forest, AR: Master Books, 2011.

Murray, Chester A. *The Authorized King James Bible Defended*. Cassville, MO: Litho Printers, 1991.

Muston, Alexis. *The Waldenses: Sketches of the Evangelical Christians of the Valleys of Piedmont*. Philadelphia: Presbyterian Board of Publication, 1853.

Nolan, Frederick. *An Inquiry Into the Integrity of the Greek Vulgate, or Received Text of the New Testament in which the Greek Manuscripts are newly classed, the integrity of the Authorised [sic] Text Vindicated, and the Various Readings Traced to their Origin*. London: R & R Gilbert, 1815.

Oard, Michael. *Frozen in Time*. Green Forest, AR: Master Books, 2006.

O'Brien, Aletheia. *Who is Gail Riplinger? A Warning for God's Sheep*. Collingswood, NJ: The Dean Burgon Society, 2010.

Origen. *On First Principles*. Translated by G.W. Butterworth. Notre Dame, IN: Ava Maria Press, Inc., 2013.

------. *The Writings of Origen: Ante-Nicene Christian Library, Translations of the Writings of the Fathers Down to AD 325, vol. X*. Edited by Alexander Roberts and James Donaldson. Translated by Frederick Crombie. Edinburgh, England: Kessinger Legacy Reprints, T&T Clark, 1989.

Packer, J.I., Merrill C. Tenney, and William White,

Jr. *The Bible Almanac*. Nashville, TN: Thomas Nelson, 1980.

Paine, Gustavus S. *The Men Behind the King James Version.* Grand Rapids, MI: Baker Book House, 1977.

Paisley, Ian R.K. *My Plea for the Old Sword.* Greenville, SC: Emerald House, 1997.

Pappas, C.H. *In Defense of the Authenticity of 1 John 5:7*. Bloomington, IN: Crossbooks, 2011.

Parker, Gary. *Creation: Facts of Life*. Green Forest, AR: Master Books, 2006.

Parker, Gary, and Mary Parker. *The Fossil Book*. Green Forest, AR: Master Books, 2004.

Paris, Edmond. *The Secret History of the Jesuits*. Ontario, CA: Chick Publications, 1975.

Postman, Neil. *Amusing Ourselves to Death*. London, England: Penguin Books, 1985.

Prothero, Donald R. Bringing Fossils to Life. New York: McGraw-Hill, 2004.

Rose Book of Bible & Christian History Time Lines. Torrance, CA: Rose Publishing, 2006.

Sanford, J.C. *Genetic Entropy and the Mystery of the Genome*. Waterloo, NY: FMS Publications, 2008.

Schoville, Keith N. *Biblical Archaeology in Focus*. Grand Rapids, MI: Baker Book House Company, 1982.

Semler, Johann Salomo, Siegmund Jakob Baumgarten, and Ferdinand Wilhelm Beer. *A Supplement to the English Universal History*. London: Rofe and Crown, 1760.

Showers, Renald E. *What on Earth is God Doing?* Bellmawr, NJ: The Friends of the Israel Gospel

Ministry, Inc., 2003.

Snelling, Andrew A. *Earth's Catastrophic Past*. Dallas, TX: Institute for Creation Research, 2009.

Sodera, Vij. *One Small Speck to Man*. Malaysia: Vija Sodera Publications, 2009.

Sorenson, David H. *Broad is the Way*. Kearney, NE: Morris Publishing, 2013.

Sorenson, David H. *God's Perfect Book: The Inspiration, Preservation, and Alteration of the Bible*. Duluth, MN: Northstar Ministries, 2009.

------. *Touch Not the Unclean Thing: The Text Issue and Separation*. 3rd ed. Duluth, MN: Northstar Ministries, 2002.

------. *Understanding the Bible: An Independent Bible Commentary*. Duluth, MN: North Star Ministries, 2008.

Starr, James W. *New Carts or Old Paths*. Greenville, SC: Truth Publishers, 2010.

Stringer, Phil. *Gail A. Riplinger's Occult Connections*. Cleveland, GA: The Old Paths Publications, 2011.

Stringer, Phil. *The Messianic Claims of Gail A. Riplinger*. Collingswood, NJ: Dean Burgon Society, 2010.

Sumner, Tracy Macon. *How Did We Get the Bible?* Uhrichsville, OH: Barbour Publishing, Inc., 2009.

Unger, Merrill F. *The New Unger's Bible Handbook*. Chicago: Moody Publishers, 2005.

Ussher, James. *The Annals of the World*. Green Forest, AR: Master Books, 2006.

Vardiman, Larry, Andrew A. Snelling, and Eugene

E. Chaffin, ed. *Radioisotopes and the Age of the Earth, Volume II: The Results of a Young-Earth Creationist Initiative*. El Cajon, CA and Chino Valley, AZ: Institute for Creation Research and Creation Research Society, 2005.

Victor, Edward, and Richard D. Kellough. *Science for the Elementary and Middle School*. Upper Saddle River, NJ: Prentice-Hall, Inc., 1997.

Waite, D.A. *A Critical Answer to James Price's King James Onlyism: 225 of Price's Statements Analyzed Carefully for Errors, Misrepresentations, and Serious Falsehoods*. Collingswood, NJ: The Bible for Today Press, 2009.

Waite, D.A. *A Warning!! On Gail Riplinger's KJB & Multiple Inspiration HERESY*. Collingswood, NJ: The Bible for Today Press, 2010.

------. *Defending the King James Bible*. Collingswood, NJ: The Bible for Today Press, 2006.

------. *The Fifth 200 Questions Answered*. Collingswood, NJ: The Bible for Today Press, 2013.

------. *The First 200 Questions Answered*. Collingswood, NJ: The Bible for Today Press, 2010.

------. *Four Reasons for Defending the King James Bible*. Collingswood, NJ: The Bible for Today Press, 1993.

------. *The Fourth 200 Questions Answered*. Collingswood, NJ: The Bible for Today Press, 2011.

------. *Heresies of Westcott and Hort (As Seen in Their Own Writings)*. Rev. ed. Collingswood, NJ: The Bible for Today Press, 2004.

------. *The Second 200 Questions Answered*. Collingswood, NJ: The Bible for Today Press, 2010.

------. *The Sixth 200 Questions Answered*. Collingswood, NJ: The Bible for Today Press, 2013.

------. *The Superior Foundation of the King James Bible*. Collingswood, NJ: The Bible for Today Press, 2008.

------. *The Third 200 Questions Answered*. Collingswood, NJ: The Bible for Today Press, 2011.

Waite, D.A., Jr. *The Doctored New Testament*. Collingswood, NJ: The Bible for Today Press, 2003.

Walton, John H. *Chronological and Background Charts of the Old Testament*. Grand Rapids, MI: Zondervan, 1994.

Walvoord, John F., and Roy B. Zuck. *The Bible Knowledge Commentary: Old Testament*. Colorado Springs, CO: David C. Cook, 1983.

Watts, Isaac. *Logic*. Grand Rapids, MI: Soli Deo Gloria Publications, 2008.

Watts, Lee. *Weighed in the Balances: A History and Comparison of Bible Versions*. Lexington, KY: God and Country Ministries, 2011.

Werner, Carl. *Evolution: The Grand Experiment*. Green Forest, AR: New Leaf Press, 2007.

------. *Living Fossils*. Green Forest, AR: New Leaf Press, 2008.

Westcott, Brooke Foss, and Arthur Westcott. *Life and Letters of Brooke Foss Westcott, D.D., D.C.L.: Sometime Bishop of Durham, vol. 1*. London: MacMillan and Co., 1903.

------, *Life and Letters of Brooke Foss Westcott, D.D., D.C.L., Sometime Bishop of Durham, vol. 2*. Reprint, London: MacMillan and Co., 1903.

Whitcomb, Jonathan. *Searching for Ropens: Living*

Pterosaurs in Papua New Guinea. Livermore, CA: WingSpan Press, 2007.

White, James R. *The King James Only Controversy*. Minneapolis, MN: Bethany House Publishers, 1995.

Williams, H.D. *The Character of God's Words is Not Found in the Septuagint*. Cleveland, GA: The Old Paths Publications, 2007.

------. *The Lie that Changed the Modern World: A Refutation of the Modernist Cry: "Poly-Scripturae."* Collingswood, NJ: The Bible for Today Press, 2004.

Wilson, Robert Dick. *A Scientific Investigation of the Old Testament*. Birmingham, AL: Solid Ground Christian Books. 1959.

Wiseman, D.J. *Chronicles of Chaldean Kings (626-556 B.C.) in the British Museum*. London: British Museum Publications Ltd., 1956.

Wiseman, Donald J., and Edwin Yamauchi. *Archaeology and the Bible: An Introductory Study*. Grand Rapids, MI: The Zondervan Corporation, 1979.

Yoder, Rodney. *The Story Behind the Versions*. Harrisonburg, VA: Christian Light Publications, 2012.

BIBLIOGRAPHY

INDEX OF WORDS AND PHRASES

INDEX OF WORDS AND PHRASES

ABOUT THE AUTHOR

Brian D. Shepherd was in the very first graduating class from Institute for Creation Research's School of Biblical Apologetics, earning a Master of Christian Education degree, with a joint major in Biblical Education and Apologetics, and a triple minor in Genesis Studies, Creation Research, and Biblical Humanities (summa cum laude, 2011). He graduated from Texas A & M University (1981) with a Bachelor of Science in Chemistry. He is also a life member of the Dean Burgon Society and on the Advisory Council. He teaches at Gatewood Baptist Church in Garland, Texas, where he lives with his wife, Phyllis and his two children, Adrian and Hannah.

CPSIA information can be obtained
at www.ICGtesting.com
Printed in the USA
FFOW05n0540230117

9 780996 807968